Here is everything you need to know to get the most Social Security checks you are entitled to—as fast as possible.

Ex Social Security claims representative (30 years with the agency) "pulls back the curtain" about what it takes to get approved for retirement, disability, SSI and Medicare.

This is an all-new, all-unique and all-original work

Cuts through the bureaucratic red tape and obfuscation and tells you in plain language what the law says and—most importantly—what the law MEANS and how it may apply to you and your situation.

You can get the legal facts from Social Security, but the language is spun by lawyers. The agency does not explain the consequences of the facts unless you have a solid background in the programs and are really good at reading between the lines.

* 2 things that delay the startup of benefit checks. The first has to do with your lifestyle, but the second can—and should be—cleared up BEFORE you file your application.

* The three questions you must ask yourself before you pick the month to retire

* What is your Full Retirement Age, and how you can get checks earlier

* If you became unable to work tomorrow, could you draw Social Security disability?

* The biggest single reasons people are denied for disability. How to avoid the one you have control over.

Get Social Security Checks

Everything You Need to File for Social Security Retirement, Disability, Medicare and Supplemental Security Income (SSI) Benefits and Get the Most Money Due You as Fast as Possible

Michael Schultz

LEGAL NOTICE

Table of Contents

Introduction

This book is intended as a guide to filing for, understanding and receiving the main benefits administered by the Social Security Administration: retirement, disability, Medicare and SSI.

The programs are complex. My job is to cut through the bureaucratic red tape and explain to you in plain language what the law means, with explanations and examples so you understand.

Frankly, a lot of this information is available for free from http://www.socialsecurity.gov , http:.//www.godirect.org, and http://www.medicare.gov . Not to mention the official Social Security Handbook and numerous pamphlets.

However, the language on all these sites is spun by teams of lawyers. It's the facts, and nothing but the facts—not the MEANING of those facts. And not suggestions on how those facts apply to you and your life. Some people are not as able to take raw facts and figure out their implications as others are.

Who This Book is For

Everybody who is in their fifties or early sixties and considering their retirement options.

People who have severe medical problems and are considering applying for disability benefits from SSA and/or SSI.

People who have already applied for such disability benefits and who are still awaiting a decision.

People on Social Security disability who want to understand better what happens if they work.

People on SSI who want to understand how their check amounts are determined.

People approaching Medicare either through age (65) or two years on disability.

People who've just suffered the death of a spouse.

Family and helpful friends of the above.

Lawyers and other representatives who genuinely wish to help their clients.

Everybody who's currently working under the United States Social Security system— (that is, almost everybody who's working inside the U.S. but not for a state or local government).

I Don't Cover Every Paragraph of the Claims Manual

I do NOT pretend this is a complete guide to every single aspect of the Social Security laws.

There are countless court cases and exceptions that apply to about 50 people in the world.

This guide will help the vast majority of SSA applicants. But it is not a replacement for guidance from an SSA Claims Representative who is familiar with your individual, specific situation.

The only complete guide is the Social Security claims manual (POMS), which is what SSA claims representatives and other employees use to make their decisions.

Life is Complicated

One reason the Social Security laws are complicated is because they try to be fair across many different kinds of people and situations. Life is complicated.

Yet that's one reason many people need some additional guidance when it comes to applying the law to your life or to your loved ones.

Everybody is different.

Very often newspaper and magazine articles about Social Security assume everybody works as an employee full time from college graduation to retirement.

That's not real life.

Adding the Human Touch—and Insider Experiences—to the Claims Manual

There is no point in me merely echoing the claims manual. I have sometimes bought one of those tax preparation books available in bookstores at the beginning of the year, researched a subject only to find that the book told me nothing the IRS didn't, and even had the nerve to refer me to the IRS! In their effort to be "complete," they cheated me. That made me quite angry, since I sure didn't buy a book on taxes just to be referred to the IRS. So I don't want to be guilty of the same thing.

Therefore, I stick to subjects where I can contribute something of value you can't find in the claims manual.

That includes clearer and expanded explanations, comments on how the regulations are applied in real life, examples, pointers on how to legally help yourself and avoid common mistakes, and some true anecdotes that pertain to the content.

I'll give you the insight of someone who worked in a Social Security field office for over thirty years. I've explained the programs to people so often I still dream of the little set speeches I gave. One of my job requirements was to tailor explanations of the law to people's level of ability to understand. I can not only explain the facts, but guide you to understand what they mean to you.

(I'll do my best. You have to think too, because I don't know you or the facts of your life. And every reader of this book will be a different person. If you were on the other side of my desk I'd be able to look at your earnings record, your Social Security benefits record (MBR) and Supplemental Security Income record (SSID). Obviously I can't do that in a book.)

Besides, the people who are paid to write the claims manual are not Claims Representatives, Benefit Authorizers or anybody else who does the actual work of the agency. They write what they're told by management to write. They don't realize how confusing some of their instructions are, or see how confusing real life can be when trying to apply the instructions to it.

If You Want Every Detail...

If you want to research every little nook and cranny of the law—and there are gazillions of them—here's the link to POMS online:

https://secure.ssa.gov/apps10/poms.nsf/partlist!OpenView

Have fun.

But remember many sections of the manual assume you have a basic working knowledge of the basics of the law. It's intended for Claims Representatives who were taught the overall big picture in a classroom setting.

If you don't already know—for example—SSI is based on income, but you start reading the income sections of the claims manual, you'll really wonder what's going on.

My CR training included reading the claims manual, but each subject began with the teacher explaining the subject first.

So in this book I've concentrated on the basics of retirement (RSI), disability (DI), SSI, and Medicare (HI).

Applying for Social Security is Not a Do It Yourself Process

Besides, I'm not so sure it's a good idea for the average person to attempt to "second guess" everything Social Security does. I don't mean accept anything wrong or which goes against POMS, but don't try to look for an error in every detail.

Even lawyers that specialize in Social Security often make mistakes when they complete the forms.

However, it is a good idea to understand the law, SSA procedures and how you can best help yourself.

But you can't be your own Claims Representative (CR) or disability counselor, nor should you try.

This book is intended to help you help your CR and your disability counselor make the best—and fastest—decision possible.

I'll define "best" as the one that gets you the most money you're lawfully entitled to.

This is especially true now the agency instructs CRs to let people enquiring about retirement choose their own month of election, without explaining what they used to always explain.

Of course, the decision as to exactly when you retire is up to you in the final analysis anyway, and I never really liked the agency's "breakeven point" explanations, but I suspect many people retiring now and in the future will come to regret their choice.

So here is a full discussion of what you need to consider before you give your boss notice you're retiring.

30 Years in the Trenches

My credential for writing this book is I was a Claims Representative in various SSA field offices for just over 30 years.

The field office is the local district or branch office where you can go in person to get a replacement Social Security card, apply for retirement benefits and so on.

That's where the rubber meets the road. Thousands of SSA employees do other important work in the Central Office Headquarters in Baltimore, the Regional Offices and the Payment Centers.

But it's field office employees who see the American people—and Teleservice Center representatives who speak to them on the telephone.

I didn't keep track of how many claims applications I took—I was far too busy. I must have taken tens of thousands, along with a large number of Continuing Disability Reviews, SSI redeterminations, representative payee accountings, and so on. Plus stuff that's important but not complicated such as Social Security numbers, change of addresses and so on.

No Shortcuts for Scammers

Notice I said above you should get all the benefits you're "lawfully" entitled to.

I hope you don't purchase this volume hoping to get insider "secrets" to benefits you're not eligible for.

I didn't spend 30 years protecting the integrity of the SSA trust funds just to help scammers now—especially when I'm drawing near to retirement age myself and don't want the trust funds drained dry by frauds.

First of all, SSA has few "secrets."

Secondly, any inside "secrets" I used to know are years out of date.

Thirdly, I no longer receive updates to the claims manual, so I didn't receive the latest "secret" memo from Central Office.

The facts I give in this book are all publicly available, just explained better than the government allows itself to. The advice is my own opinions. Others may give conflicting advice.

I can't make you eligible for benefits if you don't meet the legal requirements—and you shouldn't want to receive benefits you're not legally entitled to—but I can help you get what is legally yours.

30 Years Took Its Toll

Sometimes, you may feel as you read, I have an "attitude." Working 30 years for Social Security does that to you.

That's not just because I had to be constantly on the alert for the lies people told to try to get benefits they were not eligible for, but what people said and did that prevented them from getting benefits they were eligible for.

My job was to pay people the correct amount, and sometimes people made it harder to pay them a higher amount than a lower amount. And oftentimes they made it impossible to pay them anything at all.

The consequences of the conscious deception and the unconscious self-sabotage cut both ways.

Many people think SSA is "out to get them" and is picking on them personally.

Ridiculous. SSA employees are far too busy to "target" or single you out personally.

Most claimants are far more harmed by their own actions or failure to act in a timely fashion than by anything SSA does.

Of course, you're not one of those people, or you wouldn't be reading this book.

So let's get started.

Social Security was Intended to be Social Insurance - a Brief History

President Franklin Delano Roosevelt signed the Social Security Act August 14, 1935, setting in motion the largest—and by many measures the most successful—social welfare experiment in United States history.

The original act was comprehensive, authorizing federal money to go to the states to fund Old Age Assistance, unemployment, Aid to Dependent Children and what is now called Medicaid.

However, what most Americans think of as "Social Security" was created under Title II. And that's what I will mean in this book when I say "Social Security." (Although we'll also cover Title XVI—Supplemental Security Income or SSI—and Title XVII—Medicare.)

The concept of Social Security, generically known as social insurance, began in Europe, and was initiated in Germany in 1889. Quite a few countries began such programs before the United States.

One reason it likely passed in the US was the Great Depression was causing severe economic trauma for almost everybody, but especially the aged. Plus, many people were advocating more extreme plans to help the elderly, which were more socialistic or charitable in nature.

The concept of social insurance seemed more conservative because, although still a form of income redistribution, it also included forced savings. Workers paid for the system today so they could draw upon it when they retired in their turn.

I'm keeping this brief. Most of you probably want to know just enough to understand why the law is the way it is, so you can get what's coming to you.

However, if you're interested in more, there's a comprehensive history of Social Security on SSA's web site:

http://www.socialsecurity.gov/history/briefhistory3.html

Social Insurance, Not Socialism

Social Security was sold to the American people as a form of insurance, not welfare. Just as insurance companies offer a form of protection by spreading the cost of risk around to a large number of people, so SSA would help people meet the risk they didn't have enough money to live on when they became unable to work at age 65.

The law provided for a large percentage of the population (though not all - railroad workers, farm employees, the self-employed and government workers were not included) to pay into a government trust fund out of their paychecks, with a matching amount paid by their employer. The Social Security "Board" (now "Administration") would keep track of this money.

When a worker reached retirement age, they would draw a monthly annuity until they died.

The basic concept was the more the worker paid into the system during their work-life, the more they would receive once they retired. That's what made it insurance, not charity or welfare.

Monthly Benefit Amounts Do Not Go Up in a Straight Line

However, some bias was deliberately built in to the way benefits are calculated to help lower paid workers on the assumption they'd need the retirement benefits more than higher income workers. Yet the higher income workers did receive higher checks.

The first amount of money workers pay into the system in the year counts for more retirement money than later money.

Here's an example to make that clearer. I just made up the numbers, but the basic principle applies.

Worker A earns only $5,000 per year for forty years, then retires and gets $600 per month.

Worker B earns $20,000 per year for forty years. When they retire they do get more than Worker A, but NOT four times as much—NOT $2,400!

This is all computed for you by Social Security and not something you need to worry about. If you wish, you can read about the "bend points" here:

http://www.ssa.gov/oact/cola/piaformula.html

Somebody Has to Have Worked

The benefits have expanded during the years, but to this day, for somebody to draw a Social Security check, somebody has to have worked and earned enough to be "insured." That somebody could be yourself, your spouse or, if you're a child, your mother or your father.

Social Security is a program where the checks are earned. It is not a "needs based" form of income, which is professional jargon for welfare. This makes it distinct from a VA pension, Medicaid, food stamps, TANF, Energy Assistance, Section 8 housing assistance, and various and sundry state and local benefits paid to people because they need it.

If you (or a spouse or a parent if you're still a minor) haven't paid enough into the program, you don't get Social Security checks. It's that simple.

Another Similarity to Insurance

Furthermore, the program is similar to insurance in the sense not everybody who pays into the system—even if they're insured—will benefit from it.

For example: you're an insured worker who is still working, and you've never married and you have no children. Tomorrow you die of a heart attack.

What happens to the money you paid in to the trust funds? Nothing. It was all paid out to current beneficiaries anyway.

What happens to your right to draw benefits? They're gone, because the government can't send checks to dead people—and you left no dependents.

What if you were the sole support of your niece and nephew? SSA pays only your children. A niece and nephew are not your children. If you wanted your niece and nephew to get Social Security on your record if you died, you should have adopted them (thus making them legally your children, not your niece and nephew).

I've seen people get upset by this, and families think children should draw on a grandparent's record, and any other way around it they can think of.

But your grandchildren are not "your" children, so no, you can't arrange for them to draw your Social Security when you die.

Social Security is Targeted Taxation and Wealth Redistribution

I've heard the argument Social Security is a form of taxation, implying to receive SSA is therefore just like receiving welfare (which of course is also funded by taxes), and there's a logic to that.

However, the fact is the FICA taken out of your paycheck goes specifically to the Social Security trust funds—not to the government's general revenue fund which pays for the military, your congressperson's salary, the space program, food stamps and everything else.

The only way to get the money back is to pay enough in to be an "insured worker" (or to be directly related to one), and to meet other requirements. "Need" is NEVER one of those—at least as of April 2011. (I'll discuss the possible future of the program in a later chapter, which you can skip if you don't give a rip.)

When he retires, Bill Gates will deserve his Social Security check just as much as you do even though his net worth is about 5 billion times yours (and mine!). Someone who has spent most of their life on welfare, in jail, outside the United States, self-employed and not filing tax returns, living off their mother/boyfriend/girlfriend, living off their children's income or otherwise not paying into the system is not due a Social Security check when they retire no matter how much they "need" it—that is, how little money they have available to pay their bills—unless they're married to someone who has done the required amount of work.

In 1939 the law was expanded to cover spouses and survivors of workers. On August 1, 1956 it was greatly expanded to cover disability. And on July 30, 1965 President Lyndon Baines Johnson created Medicare as part of his Great Society.

In 1972 President Richard Nixon signed the bill consolidating state welfare programs for the aged, disabled and blind into the federal Supplemental Security Income (SSI) program. This really is not Social Security as we think of it, but it's run by the Social Security Administration and there's a close practical connection between them, especially as concerns disability.

On December 8, 2003 President George W. Bush signed the Medicare Prescription Drug, Improvement and Modernization Act of 2003 which created Part D of Medicare, to cover prescription drugs.

The Social Security System

Social Security's Headquarters—Central Office—is in Baltimore Maryland, and that's where the Commissioner of Social Security is based.

It's divided into regions: Kansas City, Denver, Philadelphia, Dallas, San Francisco, Chicago, Boston, New York, Seattle, and Atlanta.

Each of those regions has a Regional Office where the Regional Commissioner presides.

Each region is divided into areas, overseen by the Area Director. District offices and (if any) teleservice centers report to the Area Director.

This is an outmoded structure that should probably be scrapped if only to save money. Because the regions make many of their own policies, it makes for differences between the regions. Those regional and area office employees who do provide helpful services to the field offices could just as well be based in Baltimore or in a smaller local facility.

But it seemed logical in 1936 before commercial jet travel, conference calls and the Internet. Nobody has changed it yet, and the Area Directors and Regional Commissioners have no motivation to re-organize away their highly paid jobs. They close field offices as needed to save money, but don't intend to "downsize" away their own.

There're also "regions" within Central Office. One is devoted to the disability program and another one to foreign operations.

(Another false belief: you have to live in the United States to receive SSA benefits.)

Not true. Many people spend enough time in the United States working to become insured workers. When they retire or become disabled, they're just as entitled to benefits as everybody else, whether they're citizens or not, or live in the U.S. or not.

Social Security will mail checks to almost every country in the world. There are a few exceptions, such as Cuba and North Korea.

However, the system does discriminate against spouses and children who have never resided in the United States. If you're a Social Security beneficiary with a spouse and/ or children who have never resided in the United States, I advise you to check with the US embassy in their country of residence.

Each region (including disability in Baltimore) has a payment center where Social Security applications are approved, which includes getting the computer to calculate and then issue checks every month.

This too is a somewhat outmoded system. Thanks to computer improvements, field office claims representatives are getting more retirement and disability claims paid.

However, the more complex cases go to the payment centers—and they can take a long time.

(I can't tell you how to live your life, but the more spouses—ex or otherwise—you have, and the more children by the more fathers/mothers, the more your claim may be delayed. That's especially true if you don't know their current locations—their mailing address including a telephone number if possible as well as a broad location.)

It can also be delayed a lot if you've ever worked under different Social Security numbers. If you know or even think you have worked under different Social Security numbers, dig out all the paperwork and records regarding all numbers you've used and the W-2 forms you received for them all, then go to your local office and explain the situation to them right away. The sooner your work history is straightened out so it's up to date and accurate, the better.

Do NOT wait to do this until you file your claim.

Odds and Ends

Here is some basic information about Social Security and SSI benefits that doesn't really fit into the following chapters, but it's good to know, so here it is:

SSI checks come on the first of the month unless the first falls on a Saturday, Sunday or national holiday (as January 1 always does, because it is a national holiday). In that case, SSI checks are delivered on the latest available Friday.

Example: January 1 falls on a Sunday. SSI check day is Friday, December 30.

SSI checks are for that month. Therefore, the check received December 30 is for January.

****

Social Security checks used to come on the 3rd day of the month (with the same fallback provisions as SSI checks).

However, this caused a surge of telephone calls and office visits that strained the agency's work force and 800 number line capacity for the first 8 days of every month. Therefore, beginning with people who applied as of May 1997, SSA started spreading check delivery out through the month.

If your birthday falls in the first 10 days of a month, you get your Social Security check on the second Wednesday of every month. If your birthday falls within day 11 to 20th of the month, you get your Social Security check on the third Wednesday of the month. If your birthday falls in the remainder of the month, you get your Social Security check on the fourth Wednesday of the month.

That schedule avoids almost all legal holidays.

People who began getting Social Security benefits before 1997 still get their checks delivered on the third of every month.

****

Social Security checks are paid for the previous month.

Example: Ronnella was born on May 29. In September she files for retirement effective with October. Therefore, she receives her first Social Security check on the fourth Wednesday of November.

****

There is a 5 month waiting period for getting Social Security disability and Disabled Widow or Widower benefits.

Example: Larry becomes disabled in June. Therefore, the first month for which he is eligible for benefits is December. His birthday is April 15. Therefore, he gets his first check the third Wednesday of January (for December).

(That is assuming he files a claim right away and it is approved quickly. Many times people wait a long time to file. And many times it takes a long time for their claim to be approved.)

****

Social Security benefits are taxable if your total income is over $25,000 (filing as a single person)—for couples who file a joint return, it's $34,000.

****

Social Security employees operate under the Privacy Act. This means they are not allowed to reveal personal information about you except to other SSA employees or others who are part of the process, such as disability counselors of the state agencies.

They do use your name and Social Security number when requesting information on you from medical sources—you're required to sign a medical release that conforms to the HIPAA Act—and from other sources such as employers.

However, they cannot give out information on you to other people, including your family members.

Therefore, it's not a good idea to have family members go to SSA to ask questions on your behalf, unless you go with them to give your permission to discuss your case in front of you.

SSA workers are not allowed to access their own SSA records or that of any family members, or that of famous people.

Doing so will trigger computer alerts to SSA investigators and the employee will be punished.

So if you happen to know somebody who works for SSA, it's okay to ask them for generic advice, and for them to give you generic advice and information—such as this book is full of—but not to take any actions on your behalf. Go into your local office, go online or call the 800 number and do it yourself. They can get into a lot of trouble if they do anything on you directly, even just file an application for a replacement Social Security card.

They are required to safeguard your Social Security number as much as possible, and other information such as your address.

I won't say every SSA employee obeys the law to the letter, but the agency is getting stricter and stricter. Besides, some employees commit self-sabotage as well. They also do ridiculous things, get caught and pay for them, often with their jobs. And jail is not out of the question.

Also, the Privacy Act means they are not supposed to request information not required to process your application.

You have the right to refuse to answer questions or to sign required forms, but then SSA is obligated to deny your claim or suspend your checks if you're already receiving them, so what's the point?

If you want the money, you have to go through the procedures. There is a reason for all of them. You may not know what it is, and it may seem obtrusive to you, but when you're requesting the government send you money, you are giving up a certain measure of privacy, even though you didn't consent to the system in the first place.

This is especially true of SSI, because that's based on need. SSA is obligated to make sure you do meet the legal requirements, to protect taxpayers.

****

Social Security does not pay you interest for late payments. Writing the rules and determining the amounts would be a nightmare—not to mention an additional burden on the trust funds.

But this cuts both ways.

SSA also does not charge interest on overpayments due.

****

This book covers major items, such as filing for benefits. A lot of the work Social Security does from day to day, and which concerns applicants and recipients, is relatively small, but still important. That includes such things as changing your address, changing your direct deposit account, requesting replacement Social Security cards and replacement Medicare cards.

You can do all those things by visiting your local Social Security office, calling 1-800-772-1213 or visiting the agency's website. That really is easiest and fastest. And the agency is striving to be part of the 21st century trend of letting people take care of their own business online. In addition, it helps to reduce the workload burden on the field office and teleservice center staff, enabling them to focus on more important chores.

http://www.socialsecurity.gov

Meet Your Social Security Worker

I'm including this section because too many people have too many misconceptions, and when money is involved, too many people forget you catch more flies with honey than with vinegar.

The following also applies to a large extent to state agency disability officers, though you're a lot less likely to speak with them personally.

The vast majority of SSA employees are intelligent, dedicated, hard-working, professional, considerate and helpful.

They're also stressed out from overwork and worried about their jobs and their careers. They also handle more unhappy, rude people than any other profession except the police.

They want to do a good job, and try hard to do so despite the best efforts of both claimants and SSA management to stop them.

They are also trained to deal in the law (actually, the specific instructions they're given in the claims manual regarding the law) and the facts of your case.

SSA Workers are Not Congress People or Senators or the President

They don't make the law. If you have a complaint about the Social Security law, write your congressional representatives and senators. It's downright ignorant to blame SSA employees for doing their jobs correctly, which is to enforce the law as it actually is written, not as you wish it were written.

They and their families need to eat just as much as you and yours do, so don't expect them to break or bend the law on your behalf.

The best way to get what you're due from SSA is to assume the best from the people you talk to. You'll usually get it.

Be at least polite. (Moderately pleasant is best. People who acted like they were trying to be my best friend just made me suspicious.)

Most SSA Employees Want to Do the Right Thing by the Law and the Facts

Be fact oriented. Know the facts of your case. By reading this book you'll be far ahead of the average person who walks through the door, so your interview is likely to go smoothly.

I can't speak for every CR, but I for one liked people who knew what they were doing and who could answer questions. And I realized many people I spoke with were not as familiar with the program as I was, so I appreciated their questions. I especially liked questions which showed they'd been listening to what I said and thinking about it.

Sometimes CRs make mistakes, because they're human. Sometimes they misapply the law. Learning the law for your situation is your best defense against that.

Sometimes they make errors of fact.

Once I misunderstood how a life insurance policy calculated its cash surrender value, because it was not the normal kind, and I made the cash surrender value too high.

The person involved didn't scream at me. He did the smartest thing he could have. He brought in his life insurance agent, who explained to me what the policy meant (it really wasn't clearly written), so I recalculated the cash surrender value to correct my error.

If only everybody had been like him...

Why I Enjoy Lawyer Jokes So Much

Some of the worst offenders are people who fly off the handle because that's the only way they know how to react to frustration (probably not you if you're reading this book)—and lawyers.

The court system of the United States is not about discovering all the facts of a situation and then seeing how the law applies.

It's about two lawyers competing with each other.

That's what they're trained to do in law school.

And many Social Security specialist lawyers apply that confrontational approach in their dealings with the agency. It doesn't matter to them what the facts are (I've known them to make up facts when they wanted to.). And it doesn't seem to matter to them they antagonize the CRs who make decisions on their clients.

All that matters to do them is their arguments.

However, getting all the facts and seeing how the law applies to them is how CRs and state agency disability examiners are trained to think and work.

The more you give your CR and disability worker relevant facts, and the more quickly, the sooner you'll get a decision and the fairer it will be.

Working Under Social Security

So you can get a feel for the Big Picture of SSA, let's assume you're still working.

About 90% of workers in America work under Social Security. There were lots of exceptions in 1935, but a lot fewer now.

Back then, the railroad industry was made into a separate system. Now hardly anybody makes a career of working on the railroad.

Even federal employees who began in 1984 or later are covered under Social Security (and some who began before 1984 switched to that system in 1987).

The major exceptions to Social Security coverage are federal employees hired before 1984 who chose to stick with the old Civil Service Retirement System, postal workers, and state/local employees covered under their own pension systems.

Every time you're paid, 7.65% of your gross earnings is deducted from your gross pay as "FICA" taxes. FICA stands for Federal Insurance Contribution Act, and these deductions began in January 1937. They're how the Social Security trust funds gets money. 6.20% goes to the OASDI (Old Age, Survivors and Disability) SSA trust fund. 1.45% goes to the HI (health insurance or Medicare trust fund).

You don't see it, but your employee also has to "match" the amount of 7.65% when they send the money into SSA every quarter.

Officially, that money comes from the employer. Practically, you pay it all.

That's because it's all a cost to the employer of having you work for them. Your labor is worth that, or they'd reduce your wages or lay you off.

Say you make $10 per hour. The first 7.65% is deducted from that $10 gross so your check is only $9.235 (ignoring other taxes). But the employer has to send in another 7.65%, so you must be worth at least $10.765 to them (not to mention what they pay for your other benefits such as unemployment insurance). If they didn't have to pay the FICA taxes, they could pay you the full $10.765.

In 2011, the withholding rate for employees was reduced to 5.65%. That was a one-time event caused by a political deal between President Obama and Republicans in

Congress.

Quarters of Coverage

But they have to follow the law. You pay the 7.65% on your gross. Your gross is reported to the Social Security Administration every quarter.

And quarters is how it tracks your wages. They're known as quarters of coverage.

In the old days, until the late 1970s, quarters of coverage really meant calendar quarters. If you worked and earned enough to get a quarter in the June quarter—April, May and June—but you were laid off and didn't work in the September quarter, you got no coverage for the September quarter—July, August and September.

For over thirty years now, however, quarters have been determined entirely by the total amount earned for the year.

Effective 2012 (it normally goes up slightly every year), you have to earn $1,130 for one quarter.

To get a full one year (four quarters) of coverage, you must earn at least 4 X $1,130 = $4,510 within 2012. But it can be at any point in the year.

If you make $4,510 in January and then stop, you'll still get four quarters. Or if it's in December.

If you work a small job where you work through the entire year but you earn only $21.74 per week, so your total gross is just $1,130, you still get credit for only one quarter of coverage even though you worked all year long.

Now, we're talking about whether you're insured for Social Security, not how much you get.

You don't get anything if you're not insured. Being insured means having at least the minimum number of quarters of coverage.

Timing of the Quarters

The first $1,130 you make is the first quarter of the year (ending March), the second $1,130 you gross is credit for the second quarter of the year (June), the third $1,130 you gross is credited to you for the third quarter of the year (September), and the fourth $1,130 you make gives you a quarter of coverage for the fourth quarter of the year (December).

I know this seems like a minor point, and for most people it is, but for borderline cases it can make a different when deciding whether or not you're insured for disability.

FICA Limits

The requirement to pay the RSI and DI portions of the FICA taxes applies only up to a certain amount per year. As of 2012, that limit is $110,000.

That is, the 7.65% is deducted from all your paychecks until they reach that limit, and then it stops. Your employer is supposed to track that, but you ought to look carefully at your paystubs to make sure.

If your wages don't exceed that limit, you pay 7.65% on what you do make.

If you exceed the $110,000 because you work two jobs, then you'll wind up paying more FICA taxes than you're required to, and you should claim the additional amount as a tax credit on your tax return for the year. If you're an employee, you can't stop your employers from withholding what they're required to.

If you're self-employed, you know you owe 15.30% on your net earnings up to $110,000, and you must compute that on Schedule E.

However, the earnings limit doesn't apply to the 1.45% of FICA taxes that go to fund the HI Medicare trust fund. Your employer must deduct that 1.45% from all your wages no matter how high.

How to Maximize Your Social Security Benefit Amount

Earn more money under the Social Security system.

This sounds like common sense, but if you'd had my job for over thirty years, you'd know common sense is not very common.

If you work entirely or partly for cash (tips, for example - and taxi drivers), record and report all income. (Yes, you'll have to pay the other taxes too.)

If your income is cash because it's illegal, declare it and pay taxes anyway. Al Capone thought that was a crazy idea too, and he died in jail while serving time for tax evasion.

If you live off other people, work a job anyway.

Stay out of jail.

If you're in a job not covered by Social Security, get a part time job or start a part time business.

Even if your day job is covered by Social Security, get a part time job or start a part time business.

Work all the overtime you can.

Be such a good employee you're never laid off, but get promoted to higher paying jobs.

If you have a small business, report and pay your taxes on your business net income, not on what's left after you pay your personal expenses. Paying your personal expenses out of business income is not fair to employees who don't have the opportunity to evade taxes this way.

(Yes, many small business owners do treat their personal expenses as business expenses, shocking as that may be to you if you're an accountant. If you work for the IRS you probably know this even better than I do.)

Get a college degree, a postgrad degree, a certification or any other training that will qualify you for a better, higher paying job.

I know, all of the above should be common sense. But you'd be amazed at how many people spend their entire adult lives working as little as possible, or reporting as little of their earnings as possible so they don't have to pay taxes, and then complain because their Social Security check is so small or they're not insured at all.

An amazing number of people work for cash (such as domestics used to, and people in small businesses), never file a tax return and so never pay into Social Security, and then think they're entitled to a check, or a much bigger one, when they retire or become disabled.

The more you pay in, the more you'll get out.

So if you want to get more out, pay more in while you're able to.

I know—that's why "wet blanket" is my middle name.

How Much Work Makes You "Insured?"

Be Fully Insured

To receive SSA retirement benefits or disability benefits over the age of 30, you must be fully insured.

You must have earned at least 40 quarters of coverage (ten years) in your lifetime.

They can be spread out or ten years in a row. It doesn't matter. What does matter is you earned at least forty quarters.

Of course, most people earn a lot more, but forty is the minimum. The law recognizes people may spend periods unemployed for various reasons. And people the most on the margins of the labor force would be the ones who would need SSA benefits the most.

So they assumed a forty year work life and figured you should be able to work at least one-quarter (ten years) of it, or you weren't really trying and wouldn't qualify for retirement.

20/40—The Extra Requirement to get Disability

If you're over the age of thirty and you believe you're disabled, you must be fully insured and meet an additional requirement.

The framers of the disability addition to Social Security wanted to provide for workers who had paid into the system but could no longer work because they were disabled. They didn't intend the trust funds to pay people who wouldn't be working anyway.

Therefore, you must also meet what SSA workers call "twenty-forty." That means you must have worked five (20 quarters) out of the ten years (40 quarters) before you became disabled. If you don't meet that requirement, you weren't doing enough work in the years prior to your medical problem.

That makes your disability date of onset an important date, which we'll talk more about in a separate chapter.

Disabled From Age 25 to Age 30

People below age 31 can be fully insured, but would have had to work steadier than many do, so they are not expected to be fully insured, or to have worked five out of the ten years before they became disabled.

Workers in that age range must have worked three out of the six years before they became disabled.

Disabled at Age 24 or Below

These workers must have worked for a year and a half out of the three years before they became disabled.

Are You Insured for Retirement?

Most people have worked enough over their lifetimes they know automatically it adds up to more than ten years.

Others have a more spotty history, or have spent extended periods unemployed or not reporting cash income and so on.

The best way to see where you stand right now is to look at your Personal Earnings and Benefit Statement.

You did keep it, didn't you?

The Social Security Administration has been sending it once a year to everybody over age 25 for quite a few years now. They say it's aimed to arrive around your birthday. Mine usually arrives several months before.

Yet it's amazing how many people casually toss this away without even looking at it.

You can ask to be sent one by going to your local office (not recommended unless you have a lot of time to kill), calling 1-800-772-1213, or going to the website:

http://www.ssa.gov/mystatement/

It lists your entire work history under Social Security, showing the total amount you earned in each calendar year.

(Earnings not under SSA, such as working for the Post Office or the state of California, won't show up. Earnings that had Medicare deducted, but not other FICA taxes—applicable to government employers who are still under the old Civil Service system—will show up separately.)

It also lists how many quarters of coverage you earned that year. Simply add them up. If you have at least forty, you're fully insured and will be due a check when you retire.

Are You Insured for Disability?

If you're over age 30, are fully insured and worked at least five out of the last ten years before you became disabled, you are.

For most people, it's simple to figure out.

But again, if your work record is spotty, especially in the past ten years, you can figure it out on your own.

I can assure you many people worked a lot under Social Security in their late teens and twenties, then stopped or became inconsistent for various reasons.

Now that they're 45, they're fully insured but don't meet twenty forty.

Or it's not obvious.

Step 1

Determine the month you became disabled.

This can get more complicated than it sounds, and we'll discuss it in detail later. But for now, just pick a logical date. If you're not sure, pick the earliest date your medical condition began affecting your ability to work.

Let's just say it's June 2011.

Step 2

Go back to the nearest COMPLETE quarter.

The four quarters end in March, June, September and December.

So the complete quarter prior to June 2011 is the March 2011 quarter.

Step 3

Go back ten years. To the March 2001 quarter.

Step 4

Your ten year period begins with the following quarter—the June 2001 quarter.

Step 5

Count the quarters of coverage you earned from the June 2001 quarter through the March 2011 quarter.

Step 6

20 plus quarters? If so, you're insured for disability for a date of onset in the June 2011 quarter. (Could be April, May or June).

Under 20 quarters? You're not insured for Social Security disability. If your other income and resources are low enough, however, you can apply for SSI.

Notice that if in 2001 you made enough money for only one quarter of coverage, that quarter is assumed to be the March 2001 quarter and doesn't count as part of this calculation.

That's why I said that could be important for borderline cases.

If You're Under Age 30

The same basic process applies to counting quarters: only if you're aged 25 through 30 you must have three years worth of quarters—12—in the six years prior to your disability date of onset.

If you're aged 24 or less, you must have one and a half years worth of quarters—6—in the three years prior to your disability date of onset.

Now let's assume you're getting up in age, you're not disabled and you've got at least forty quarters of coverage (so you're fully insured).

Examples:

1. George is 58. He's worked the last 35 years straight for IBM. He has a heart attack and his doctor tells him not to return to work. Is he insured?

Easily. 35 X 4 = 140 quarters, not even counting any work he did as a teenager, in college or part-time. He's fully insured and worked ten out of the ten years before his heart attack.

2. Same situation, only this George has taught at Houston High School for 35 years without any part-time jobs or businesses. Is he insured?

No way. Teachers are under local pension systems, not Social Security. He must file for whatever disability benefit the Houston Public School System provides its teachers.

3. Jerry is 35. He worked ten years for McDonald's, then spent two years in jail for possession of a controlled substance. He just got out and alleges he became disabled in jail because of all the stress he suffered there. Is he insured for disability?

He worked 10 full years so he meets twenty forty, so he is fully insured. Out of the last ten years, he worked eight (missing only the two years he spent in jail).

Therefore, he is insured for disability.

4. Same situation, but this time Jerry worked his ten years for McDonald's starting at age 16. At age 27 he left the straight world and began supporting himself as a drug dealer (without reporting his earnings or paying FICA and other taxes on them). Is he insured for disability?

No. He still worked 10 years and therefore is fully insured. So if he survives to age 62, he can draw retirement Social Security benefits. However, in the last ten years he's worked only one or two, so he does not meet twenty forty.

If has no other income and resources, he can apply for SSI.

Should or can you retire now—or later?

Filing for Retirement

Again assuming you're fully insured, you can retire at age 62. That is the minimum age for receiving Social Security retirement benefits.

But should you?

That's a complex decision that depends on your answers to three questions. You'll have to decide for yourself:

1. How much money do you need or want to live on, and how much—if any—income will you (including your spouse if any) be receiving besides Social Security? How much of an investment portfolio do you have saved up? How much income does it produce for you?

(And it's important to notice whether you think in terms of what you "need" to live on or what you "want" to live on. Some people are content with the minimum. Others want more. Which are you?)

2. How much do you love or hate your job, and how much do you want the changes retirement would bring?

Some people's self-identity is tied in to their work. Some wives don't want their husbands at home during the day. Some people have hobbies they wish to pursue full-time. Some people can continue doing work they love on a part-time basis, or as a contract consultant instead of a full-time employee. Obviously that ties in to income as well as lifestyle.

3. How is your health and general physical and mental ability to work?

I specified that you're not disabled. However, "not disabled" doesn't rule out having health problems that make it increasingly difficult or unpleasant for you to work, or the expectation of them coming soon.

Some 85 year olds still feel like they're 25 and run ultra-marathons. Some 60 year olds feel 100 and are on the edge of death.

There's one unfortunate general rule of thumb:

The more you need to know EXACTLY how much your monthly benefit will be, the more you need to keep working.

If you can't pay your bills unless you get more than $1,203 a month, the more of a risk you're taking by retiring.

The people who can afford to retire have a large portfolio with a high income from dividends and interest. And perhaps a private pension in the family. Or they have a blog that makes four figures a month from Google Adsense. And their house is paid for.

In other words, they're not depending on their Social Security check to survive.

Of course they want what they've earned, but they won't miss any meals if their monthly check is $25 less than they estimated.

Bear in Mind The Cost of Living Raises That are Not Happening

In 1976, because of the high inflation of that era, Congress passed a law mandating annual cost of living allowance (COLA) increases for Social Security beneficiaries so their incomes would go up as their living expenses increased.

The increases are based on the Consumer Price Index (for urban wage earners) the federal government computes every year. However, quite a few years ago they stopped counting increases in the price of food and energy, with the rationalization these expenses can fluctuate a lot based on short-term (that is, noninflationary) factors.

That's true. However, what happens if there is general inflation in those two items, but not in the rest of the economy?

Retirees can cancel that cruise. They can put off buying new clothes. They can scale down what they give to their grandchildren.

But they have to pay their heating bills and buy food. The two expenses most important to everyone on a fixed income are the two expenses the government doesn't even try to help you keep up with.

Social Security beneficiaries received a COLA increase every year from 1977 through 2009. However, the overall trend is inflation is down. We're a long way from the traumatic 70s.

Interest rates can't go much lower until they hit zero. Home prices are greatly reduced from their 2007 peak.

But as I write oil is hitting $4 and more a gallon, and food companies are warning of major increases in the price of food.

Yet Social Security beneficiaries are currently being forced to live on the same amounts they received in 2009.

NOTE: Effective 2012 there's a 3.6% COLA raise.

And in case you haven't noticed, there is no political momentum for raising government expenses. Just the opposite.

Retiring at Age 62—the Catch

I wrote you can retire at age 62—or 63, or 64 or at any age before you full retirement age—(assuming fully insured status), but I didn't mention the catch.

If you choose to retire "early" (before your full retirement age), Social Security will calculate how much your full retirement monthly rate would be if you were that age—and then reduce it.

Up to the first 36 months you retire before your full retirement age, your check gets reduced 5/9ths of 1% for each month. That doesn't sound like much, but it adds up.

This means if you retire exactly three years before you've reached your full retirement age, your check amount will be reduced exactly 20%.

Thanks to increasing the full retirement age past age 65, it's possible to have your check reduced by more than 20%.

If you retire 37+ months prior to your full retirement age, your check will be reduced 5/12ths of 1% for every month over 36 months.

Some People Believe This Reduction Lasts Only Until They Reach Full Retirement Age - These Same People Also Believe in Tinkerbell

That reduction is permanent. Contrary to some people's wishful thinking, your check will NOT be increased once you reached your full retirement age. If that were true, it'd be stupid not to draw SSA at age 62.

Once you take early retirement, your check will go up only:

1. For annual COLAs.

2. You return to work and earn additional quarters of coverage that raise the amount you're eligible for.

3. You withdraw your early retirement application and repay all the benefits you've received. And then don't file again until you reach your full retirement age. (Legal and

possible, but not often used, for the obvious reason not many people can afford to repay those benefits or they wouldn't have taken them in the first place.)

So you should think long and hard about all the consequences before you file for early retirement.

The Breakeven Point Analysis

For many years, CRs would help people make that decision by calculating their "breakeven" point.

People who take early retirement obviously get more money right away than people the same age who wait until they reach full retirement age.

So there is an immediate, short-term advantage. 80% of your full benefit is much more money than no check.

In the long run, however, people who wait get more money, because their monthly checks—when they do start coming—are higher.

So CRs used to figure out how many years it would take for the full retirement age retiree to "catch up" and surpass the early retiree.

Then people would see how they felt about that and decide accordingly.

Example:

Lois files for RIB exactly 36 months prior to her full retirement age. Her full benefit would be $1,000, so she gets $800 ($1,000 minus 20%) monthly.

Her twin sister Laura waits until she reaches her full retirement age, and then starts drawing $1,000 a month.

For twelve years, Lois will have received more money than Laura.

After twelve years, however, Laura gets more money.

If you're 62 and in poor health and you're told you'll be ahead of the game for 12 years if you retire now, that may sound like a long time, especially if you expect to die before then anyway. (And maybe you will.) So in that case, early retirement may be a good choice for you.

This is especially true for people who have been fired or laid off and are close to losing unemployment benefits.

In this financial crisis, I'm sure many people have taken early retirement who had planned to work to their full retirement age.

You may be the kind of person who's determined to live to 100, and the kind of person who wants all you can get. So you wait until your full retirement age.

This is a good idea for you especially if you're still working and you're lucky enough to enjoy your work.

What Social Security has Never Told People

There's an additional argument for taking reduced money now rather than later.

Money has what's called a "time value." That's why you're paid interest on your savings account. You are giving up the present use of your money, so you must be compensated.

And when you borrow money, you must pay interest on it.

To make a truly sophisticated analysis of your retirement options, you'd have to analyze the time value of every choice.

You could certainly do it with a spreadsheet program, but frankly in my opinion that's overkill.

And you still could not make a 100% accurate determination because it requires feeding in interest rates, and you can't know what interest rates will be next year or five years from now, so you'd have to estimate.

Just remember a check in your hand is worth two in the bush. It's one part of the analysis, but not a big part.

Determining Check Amounts

So you know the more that you pay in, the more you get back. How does that work exactly?

When you file for retirement, SSA looks at your entire earnings record. That is, all the money employers reported on you for your entire life.

However, it will not include:

Wages that employers should have reported but didn't. That's a good reason for keeping your annual W-2 forms and checking your annual Personal Earnings and Benefit Statement to make sure all your new earnings show up there. That's especially true if you worked for a small business that may not have had the cash to pay its obligations—especially if they went out of business during or after your employment.

Self-employment if you didn't file a Schedule C and Schedule E and report it. This also includes unreported tips for you waiters and waitresses.

Working for state and local governments.

Working for the Post Office.

Nor does it include work under federal civil service prior to 1984. Or if you're a federal employee hired before 1984 who remained under the old civil service law rather than switch to FERS.

Then they take each amount, apply each year's cost of living raise to it, until they've calculated its value in terms of current dollars.

You don't need to think about this or attempt it yourself. I sure wouldn't.

The concept just means if you made $355.85 working for McDonald's in 1969, SSA will see what that is worth in current dollars (the year you are actually applying).

That just provides a way to fairly compare wage amounts year by year, because we all know the value of the US dollar has been going down. In 1969 $355.85 was not a fortune but it was a decent amount to earn when the minimum wage was all of $1.30 per hour.

I don't know exactly what that will be when converted in the dollars of the year you retire, but it will be a lot more than $355.85.

After they make all your earnings comparable, they keep the thirty-five years you made the most money—the "high 35."

You can increase your monthly checks by continuing to work after retirement.

Let's say your 1969 work for McDonald's is part of your High 35 years, but after you retire you return to McDonald's as a manager and make a lot more money than in 1969.

Later, SSA will recalculate your High 35. 1969 will be dropped off, and 20XX will be added. They'll recalculate your benefit amount and start paying you more.

Another Way to Increase Your Retirement Benefits

To encourage people to continue working as long as they can, SSA will increase your benefits if you delay taking retirement past your full retirement age.

Your benefit amount will be raised 2/3rds of 1% per month—8% annually—for every month you delay filing for RIB after attaining your full retirement age.

That's until you reach age 70.

Once you reach age 70, there is NO advantage in waiting. File for RIB.

What About Work After Drawing RIB Benefits?

Back to basics—Social Security is a social insurance program to insure you against the risk of not having any money when you get old. It's not a reward or compensation for reaching 65 or any other age.

Therefore, years ago you had to meet a retirement test. If you were making too much money, you weren't really retired and so couldn't draw SSA.

The details of all that have changed over the years.

Now it's actually gone, except for taking reduced retirement benefits.

Once you reach your full retirement age or later, there are no restrictions on how much money you can make from a job or business. That's up to you, your employer, and so on.

That's true at no matter what age you retire. Once you reach your full retirement age, there are no restrictions on your earnings.

But from age 62 up to your full retirement age, SSA will allow you to earn only a small amount until your checks must be reduced.

The exact amount goes up a little every year. In 2012 it's $14,640.

If you are drawing RIB in 2012 and are still below your full retirement age, you're working and you make under $14,640 total for the year, there is no effect on your eligibility.

However, what if you make $15,000? What happens?

Once you go over the $14,640 mark, you are overpaid $1 for every $2 you are over.

SSA will perform this simple calculation:

15,000 - 14,640 = $360

You are $360 over the limit.

360 / 2 = $180

Because of the overpaid $1 for every $2 over procedure, your overpayment is half of the money you went over the limit. That's why I divided by two.

You will be sent an overpayment letter for $180.

Once you know you're working and that you expect to make over $14,160, you should report that to SSA. They can reduce your monthly checks based on your expectation.

In the year you reach your full retirement age, the limit is $38,880. If you go over that, you're overpaid $1 for every $3 over.

Example:

Harry's full retirement age is 66. He turns 66 on October 3, 2012. In that year he grosses a total of $41,589. He is overpaid:

41,589 − 38,880 = $2,709

2,709 / 3 = $903

He is sent an overpayment notice for $903.

From 2013 on, there is no limit on what he can make, because he's reached the full retirement age.

Example:

Mary retires at age 63 because she was laid off. Then she finds a new job, and the next year (2012) makes $80,000. In that same year, her monthly benefit amount is $1,200. However, she decides not to report her new job to Social Security because, after all, she worked hard for that money.

She's later shocked when she receives an overpayment letter for $14,400—every dime she received in 2012. Why?

80,000 - 14,400 = $65,600

65,600 / 2 = 32,800

She's not overpaid $32,800 because she didn't receive that much. Her total benefit amount for the year was $14,400, so that's her overpayment.

When she found her new job she would have been best off to withdraw her RIB application (albeit that requires repaying all benefits received).

If she couldn't afford to refund it all, she should still have reported her new job to SSA and worked things out.

As it is, she'll file for a waiver but be denied because she is at fault for not reporting the change and someone making $80,000 per year should be able to make monthly payments.

(Bear in mind most CRs make under $80K per year, and have just gotten their first Cost of Living Allowance raise since 2009. If you have to pay your bills on less than that, how would you feel about someone else asking for charity from the taxpayers (such as yourself)?

What is Your Full Retirement Age

Year Born	Full Retirement Age
1938	65 + 2 months
1939	65 + 4 months
1940	65 + 6 months
1941	65 + 8 months
1942	65 + 10 months
1943 - 1954	66
1955	66 + 2 months
1956	66 + 4 months
1957	66 + 6 months
1958	66 + 8 months
1959	66 + 10 months
1960 on	67

*** Attention you New Year babies born on January 1. You "attain" your full retirement age on December 31 of the preceding year, so if—for example—you were born January 1, 1955, your full retirement age is 66. ***

So the upshot is, you still have to squarely face your needs and desires, and your personal situation.

As you saw from Mary's example, if you are still working and plan to make more than double your payment amount plus $14,160, you won't be due anything anyway.

If you think you can make around $14,160 or only a little over, then work and early retirement fit well together for you.

If you want to work and make as much as you want without worrying about a limit of only $14,160, then you're better off waiting to file until you can't work or you reach your full retirement age, whichever comes first.

If you hate your job and are financially secure, there's no reason to wait. This is even more true if you want to pursue some hobby or passion, especially if you may be able to monetize it.

Maybe your passion is mountain climbing. Start a blog and it can defray your climbing expenses.

But some people love their careers, so they may as well keep working, because they enjoy it.

Many people want to quit one job so they can work another one they enjoy more even if it doesn't pay as much. Or start a little business. Or to volunteer their services at the local hospital.

However, the more economically frightened and insecure you are, the more you need to keep working even if you hate your job.

Before I retired from SSA, I went to several retirement seminars the agency gives to employees who are getting up in age, so they can start planning their futures.

There was a lot of useful information, but when the presenter started going through some tedious health insurance factors, my eyes glazed over.

I wanted to know about my health insurance, but didn't want to worry about the premiums down to the last fifty cents.

If you have to detail all your expenses down to the last cup of coffee, or you won't be able to pay all your bills and will worry about becoming a bag lady, then you better keep your day job.

And as already mentioned, you cannot predict your future bills anyway. Food and energy are going up, but how far up remains to be seen.

If You're At Least 62, Below Your Full Retirement Age and Believe You're Disabled

You can file for disability at any point up to your Full Retirement Age. After that, it doesn't matter. You get the full amount of monthly benefits simply because of your age, so the agency is not going to pay for a disability decision on you.

Many people stop work prior to their Full Retirement Age, file for early RIB—they must be at least 62 years old—and also file for DIB.

SSA will get your early, reduced RIB check started right away (assuming it's easy to verify your date of birth which it is, these days, for most applicants). Your DIB claims will be processed just like any other DIB claim, usually taking longer, maybe very much longer.

But if you eventually are found to be disabled, your monthly benefit amount is raised to the full amount just as though you have attained your Full Retirement Age.

I wouldn't advise applying for DIB just for the heck of it, but if your medical condition really is a problem for you, then you should.

The worst that can happen is SSA denies your DIB claim and you just continue to get the reduced RIB checks.

If you have mountains to climb and can afford to...get to it!

Disability 101

"Disability" is a broad term. For this book, it can mean both Social Security—Title 2 (DIB), Disabled Adult Child (DAC) and Disabled Widow(er) (DWB)—and SSI disability.

When I want to refer only to someone receiving Title 2 on their own earnings record, I'll use the term DIB.

Some people use the term "SSD." I suppose it's short for "Social Security Disability," but it's not an acronym anybody in the agency uses. It's used by lawyers, social workers, and some claimants.

It's also possible to be a disabled widow or widower and draw on the record of your deceased spouse if you do so within 7 years of the date of their death and you are disabled. These are DWB—Disabled Widow(er) Benefits.

And if you're the adult child of a wage earner who is disabled, retired or deceased (and who died while insured) and you became disabled before age 22 and have never married, you can get Disabled Adult Child (DAC) benefits on that parent's record.

And when I refer to SSI, I'll specify SSI. And I'll specify when I mean SSI for children.

Basic Definition of Disability

A medical condition—or combination of conditions—which:

1. Are expected to result in death within 1 year OR

2. Make you unable to perform substantial gainful activity (SGA will be covered in a future chapter.) for at least one year.

Medical conditions are understood to be diagnosable by doctors. Of course, this is easier for some conditions than others.

But it means you can't just walk into an SSA office, say you feel too bad to work and get approved automatically.

It requires medical documentation.

People who meet the first requirement are rare, but they exist and you can only feel sorry for them. Generally, by the time they reach SSA they have a lot of medical sources.

Social Security is Permanent Disability

One source of great conflict and disappointment is the failure of people to understand disability benefits from Social Security are for "permanent" medical conditions—defined as at least one year.

Sometimes people apply for things like accident injuries and broken arms—medical problems from which they should recover within one year. Sometimes they even say things such as, "Once I'm out of this cast I'll go back to work," but insist on filing a useless claim.

Then they get upset when they're denied, even though SSA explains up front the basic definition and requirement of getting disability through SSA.

It's a bad situation also because if someone is not able to work—even temporarily—they're not eligible for unemployment benefits either.

(Though that doesn't stop many people from receiving them anyway if they can conceal their medical problems. Many SSA disability applicants receive unemployment while they're waiting for the agency to process their disability applications.)

All I can do is advise you of several things:

1. Before this happens to you, follow the advice of personal finance experts who tell you to have a 3 to 6 month emergency fund so you can pay bills if something does happen to you.

2. Check with your local welfare agencies. Some states, counties or municipalities have temporary disability benefits available.

3. If your job has sick leave, build up your balance. As a federal employee, I knew people who seemed to get sick every time their sick leave balance was up to eight hours. If they later had a real, long-term medical problem, they had no income.

4. If you don't have such sick leave on your job, take out disability insurance. There are private companies that will provide this. Check with an insurance agent.

(I know the idea of paying for their own medical or disability insurance shocks some Americans, who now think it all should be paid for either their employer or the government, but it is still available. Do without a few fast food meals and pay the premium. Before I worked for the government, when I was making only the minimum wage, I paid for my own medical insurance.)

The person alleging disability is evaluated by a number of factors. Obviously it includes their medical condition. It also includes their age, education, and work history.

Here's an example:

Harry and John both have equally severe heart attacks on the same day. When they recover, they both go into SSA to apply for DIB.

However, although Harry and John have equal medical problems, they are very different people.

Harry is 61 years old, has a 5th grade education and has always worked unskilled construction jobs—manual labor.

John is 25, has a Masters in Accounting, and has worked several years for a CPA firm.

Who do you think has the best chance of being approved?

Neither has a guarantee. They could both be denied. They could both be approved. But Harry has the best chance because of his high age, low education and physically demanding work history.

Your Medical Condition or Combination of Impairments

Unlike old made for TV movies, people rarely have one problem at a time. Some people in wheelchairs are alcoholics as well. People with schizophrenia can also have high blood pressure.

Sometimes a totally healthy young adult will break their leg or something. However, most claims involve a combination of impairments.

You Can't Pick and Choose Impairments to "File For"

Every so often I had someone complain to me the state agency was asking them about a condition they didn't "file for." In their own mind, they filed for their depression but not their high blood pressure (for example).

You file for disability benefits, not for a particular disease. The state agency is required to evaluate your entire medical condition, including all physical and all mental impairments.

You'll be asked for every medical condition that affects your ability to work.

Even if something is minor, you should include it if it affects you.

For instance, you have some minor arthritis in your left shoulder but you're filing because you were in a bad car accident. List the arthritis and precisely how it bothers or limits you. Added to your major problems, it may (or may not) make a difference. But the disability examiner can't consider it if they don't know about it.

You May Not Be Approved for What You Think

Once I took a disability application for a guy who alleged he had a bad back.

Two weeks later the state agency worker called me and told me she was approving him for a presumptive disability payment.

"What the—you mean the guy with a bad back?"

"Before I could process his denial, he was in a terrible car accident. Now he's in ICU."

Can You Get Disability Checks for X Condition?

I used to hear that question pretty often, and if you think about life, it's a very simplistic question.

The answer is—it depends.

How severe is the condition FOR YOU?

Is a cut on your arm serious?

Not if it's a tiny paper cut that heals in ten minutes.

But if your arm has been chopped into by an axe and your arterial blood is squirting sky-high, you're about to die.

So nobody can say you are disabled because you have high blood pressure, depression, arthritis, heart disease or even cancer.

It depends on how serious YOUR case is, and how it affects you bearing in mind your age, education and work history as explained above.

If you don't feel your high blood pressure if you take your medicine as your doctor tells you to do, you're probably not disabled barring other conditions.

But if you get dizzy and over-heated every day, it's affecting you.

If your high blood pressure has already destroyed one of your kidneys so you're on a dialysis machine three times a week, you'll be approved.

The Medical Decision is Done by the State Agency—Not Social Security or Your Doctor

The Social Security Administration does not make decisions based on medical evidence. That is done by a state agency.

When the Social Security disability act was passed 45 years ago, the lawmakers felt having SSA make its own medical decisions would be a conflict of interest. Therefore, it required every state to set up an agency to make these decisions.

So your state agency worker is an employee of your state government, not SSA. CRs collect the information at the initial interview, then forward it to the state agency.

The state agency requests medical records from your treatment sources. The worker makes the final decision about whether you're disabled or not, and it's signed off on by a doctor.

Social Security accepts whatever the decision is.

State agency workers have a complex job, because they have to know a lot about diseases, medicines, tests and so on. They have to keep up with advances in medical treatments and new drugs. They have to be able to compare the medical facts of your case to the criteria set by the regulations they must follow.

We Want Your Doctor's Medical Opinion of You, Not Their Vocational Opinion

Sometimes people have been told by their doctors to stop working, and they don't understand why SSA just doesn't accept that statement and pay them.

Your doctor is trained in medicine and their medical specialty. They're not an expert in Social Security disability legal requirements. And they are not vocational experts.

SSA wants to know the medical facts from your doctor, and test results, and their medical opinion, diagnosis and prognosis.

Certainly the state agency worker uses all that information as part of the decision process. But the decision whether you're disabled is up to them, not your doctor.

Every Claim is Different Because Every Person is Different

Social Security evaluates every claim separately on its own merits, and approves or denies them based on the evidence (sometimes the lack of evidence) available.

Some people believe that SSA automatically denies claims. That's ridiculous and insulting—simply not true.

Over half of all initial claims are denied. That means a significant number are approved.

Of the ones that get denied, some of them will be approved eventually on appeal (we'll discuss appeals in a later chapter).

One reason some claims get denied at the initial claims level but approved upon appeal is the claimant doesn't take the process seriously enough. They think they can just waltz into the SSA office, give answers off the top of their heads and receive a check next week. In their own minds they deserve the check so much they don't realize SSA needs concrete and objective evidence.

They don't give all the information they could. They don't submit all the evidence and forms they could. They fail to attend their consultative exam.

That last one is a very big one.

Most disability applicants do not have enough medical evidence available to be approved or denied. So the state agency sets up an appointment for them with a doctor who contracts to perform the necessary tests and examination.

If they fail to keep that appointment—which happens a lot—they're denied.

However, something about that initial claims denial letter seems to slap some cold water on their faces, and they realize SSA takes the process very seriously and if they want that government check, they better start taking it seriously too. So they file an appeal, keep the consultative exam and get approved.

Others will have their denial upheld on appeal because their medical conditions simply aren't serious enough to meet the criteria of the law.

You can argue with Congress about this, but I doubt they'll be making disability easier to get any time soon.

Many other people think they should get disability for obviously trivial conditions (my favorite was "hammer toes"). They get denied, realize it's not that easy, that they don't qualify, and go to work.

By investing in this book, you've shown you do take the process seriously. If you follow my advice, you'll give yourself the best chance possible. I still can't make any guarantees—I don't know you or your medical problems—but if you are prepared, and supply everything you're asked for, and go to your consultative exam, you have the best chance possible.

Substantial Gainful Activity (SGA)

I mentioned before one reason laws get so complicated is they're trying to deal with life and people, and life and people are complicated.

Social Security's general idea of "disability" is you "can't work," and that's how most of us speak of it much of the time.

However, that's too simplistic. Because as soon as they pass a law saying you can't work to be disabled, there'll be somebody who says, "So you're going to deny my claim because I work one hour a month for the minimum wage, even though I have the following diseases?"

Obviously it makes common sense to say if someone can work one but only one hour per month for the minimum wage, they are disabled. They're not able to support themselves on that.

But then somebody else will be working two hours, somebody else three, and so on, until people working forty hours a week plus overtime for $100 per hour would be applying for disability.

Somebody has to draw a line in the sand.

For disability, that line in the sand is called Substantial Gainful Activity (SGA).

If you are still working but you go into a Social Security office to apply for disability, the first thing the CR will be asking you is how much money you're making at your job, and how much you spend on medicine or other disability-related expenses.

Based on what you say, they'll compute your average monthly wages.

If you get paid monthly, that's easy.

If you get paid semi-monthly, they multiply that amount by two.

If you get paid once a week, they'll multiply your weekly gross by 4 1/3. (That's how many weeks are in a month.)

If you get paid once every two weeks, they'll multiply your biweekly gross by 2 1/6.

Then they'll deduct what you spend on medicine and other impairment related expenses.

If you have trouble giving them this information—most people know how much they make an hour, but you'd be amazed at how many don't know the number of hours a week they work—or they're skeptical (if you're accountant at a CPA firm they probably won't believe you work only 10 hours a week for minimum wage), or if your work schedule varies (the norm in many industries, especially fast food), they should ask to see your paystubs for at least the last few months.

Also, the expenses must be related to the condition you believe is disabling. Getting a prescription drug for bronchitis when your disability is cancer does not count.

If you have trouble coming up with your medical-related expenses, they'll want to see the receipts. Not having been bothered to keep them will not help you.

Subsidies

What if you believe your employer is giving you what SSA calls a "subsidy?"

In essence, that means knowingly paying you more than you're worth.

Examples could be allowing you lower production than other workers of your job type and wage level, more frequent rest breaks, extra support, fewer or easier duties etc.

In real life, most businesses don't go along with this. You may be working for an old friend or a family member who tolerates this from you but nobody else. If so, and you need this to be below SGA, bring them or a specific letter from your employer.

"Mary Lou works forty hours a week for me and I pay her $10 per hour. However, that's because she's worked for me a long time and I feel sorry for her since she became ill. She only produces ten widgets an hour now, so she is really worth only $8 per hour."

Frankly, these are relatively rare unless a specific vocational rehabilitation program is involved. I've seen people working at McDonald's and as baggers in supermarkets who have obvious mental disabilities. I believe the employer gets some kind of tax break or other economic benefit from employing them.

One indicator of subsidy is if you have a job coach. Job coaches get paid more per hour than the work the people they are coaching perform is worth, so that's a big subsidy.

However, people in these programs are already in the system, and probably have been getting SSI for years before they go to work.

SGA for the Self-Employed

If you run a business, SGA is not always so easy to determine. A lot depends on the kind of business, how much work you put into it and of course what you're netting now.

Officially, there are 3 "tests." I believe most CRs focus on the first one, because the other two are tough to determine.

First they will look at both the amount of income you receive and how much effort you currently put into your business.

The CR will have access to what net profit you've reported for your business in previous years, assuming you have made a net profit and reported it to the IRS. (And if you allege being supported by your business for years but you didn't file a tax return, that right there will tell the CR that you're not to be trusted. You're one of those people who doesn't want to pay taxes when times are good, but you come to the government (and taxpayers) with your hand out for money when you're disabled or want to retire.)

(NOTE: if you don't want to pay taxes, I don't blame you. But to evade taxes ethically you have to assume responsibility for yourself. Take a portion of your profits, invest them and then live on that for the rest of your life. I'm not saying it's easy. Most people have a hard time with it, and that's why Social Security was set up to begin with. But it's not fair to want to have it both ways. To evade taxes now yet want taxpayer money later in life. Still, many people do just that.)

(SECOND NOTE: this failure to report and pay all taxes on self-employment income can keep somebody from being insured (unless they have forty quarters of coverage from actual employment)—and it DOES lower their actual benefit amount. You get credit for what you pay into the system, not on what you fail to report. However, these people then often qualify for SSI, which is taking money directly from taxpayers, so they are still ripping off the system. Yet I've heard them complain about how little they get after a lifetime of working so hard. Hard work doesn't count. Paying into the system does.)

If your business consists basically of you providing services (as a doctor, an accountant, a plumber, a lawn care provider etc), you must be providing significant services to the business. Even if you employ others to help you, you basically are the business.

If your business is a larger operation, then you need to document your contributions. Generally, if you work 15 or more hours a week in the business, that's considered substantial.

(I'm sure many self-employed people will laugh at that. 15 hours a week would sound like a vacation to many. However, that is SSA's standard.)

If you are putting in that 15 hours or more and your net earnings from self-employment are above the current SGA level, then you're performing SGA and not eligible for disability.

If you're performing significant services but your net income is under SGA, then the CR will probably just go ahead and take your claim, especially if you can detail changes and explain them in terms of your medical condition.

Maybe last year you netted $50,000, but you were healthy then. Since your accident you've been able to work only 8 hours a week and your income has gone down correspondingly.

If your business—or your participation in it—has gone down recently due to your medical condition, be ready to explain that in enough detail to be credible.

Maybe you used to be one of those business owners who opened the place up in the morning, closed it at night, then made the bank deposit, then went home and did the paperwork. But you can't do that anymore, so you've hired new employees or something.

Now you go in for a few hours to keep things running right, then go home and go to bed.

Be very clear and precise about these details.

If your business is a corporation, it'll be easier to believe others could replace you, but SSA employees have seen a lot of small business owners, including those who own controlling interest in the stock of private corporations, who claim they're retired or disabled, but are still on the business premises 25 hours a day.

There are two other "tests" of SGA for business owners: comparability of work and worth of work activity.

Comparability of work means you're performing SGA if you net what other people in your business make in your local area.

If that doesn't make sense, it's because it does make sense, but is difficult to determine. If you own a barber shop, net $990 a month and put in 15 hours a week, I'm going to say you're performing SGA because I know every other barber in the city makes the same amount?

How can that be documented? I could call the other barbers but they have no reason to even talk to me. They have businesses to run. Maybe they'll lie. Maybe they have more income than they want to admit to, or will want to brag. Besides, I'm sure they're working more than 15 hours a week to pay their bills.

SSA employers do have access to earnings records, but not on a casual basis, and not without a full name and date of birth. Why should a barber tell me that information to help out a competitor?

And even if they do, would that tell me what they're going to make this year?

What if you were checking out mortgage brokers in 2008 based on their 2007 tax returns? There'd be a big difference just because of the economy.

Worth of work activity means even if you're not making as much as the other barbers in your area, if you would have to pay an employee to do the same work more than SGA, then you're performing SGA.

Say you're making $700 a month as full-time barber. If you had to pay an employee $1,100 to perform all your duties, then you're performing SGA.

In practice, no CR want to hold fake employment interviews to document what wages prospective barber shop employees will demand.

Besides, except for certain highly paid professions, and especially in bad economic times, there's always somebody ready to undercut somebody else for a job if they need it badly enough.

In practice, the CR will go mainly by your net income and if you allege putting in less than 15 hours a week (but most will be suspicious of this.)

In practice, self-employed people either make far more than SGA, or they're barely scraping by. I had many people who did odd jobs, cut hair, sold Avon and stuff like that on an irregular basis.

Many never saw $1,000 in their best month.

Self-Employment is Not Where All SSA Employees Shine

Most CRs are very bright people, but they are government employees. That doesn't mean they have no entrepreneurial background. Some do, but most don't. Newer CRs especially can be thrown off by the difference in mindset. More experienced ones will not. (But the more experienced CRs will be the most skeptical of your allegations of putting in under 15 hours per week, so you will need to explain that in detail to them.)

I say this because nobody understands your business like you do, and so don't assume the CR knows how it works as well as you. You may have to explain a lot to the CR.

But do not also assume they're stupid just because they're a government employee.

(I once had somebody admit a clever, sophisticated fraud to me, because he assumed I wouldn't understand the implications of his answers to my questions. Fortunately for the DI trust fund, I did. Although I believe they decided not to prosecute him, they did stop paying him the Social Security checks he was not eligible for.)

Some CRs don't have a clear understanding of the difference between being an employee and self-employed.

Once a woman came into our office alleging she was disabled, but supporting herself by working as a prostitute. The (new) CR asked me on how to handle it.

I told her to get the woman's best estimate of her average monthly net—and the new CR freaked out.

"Oh, yeah, right. How am I going to send a 4201 (wage verification letter) to every man she's slept with?"

I tried to explain prostitutes are not employees (maybe they are in the area of Nevada where it's legal - I don't know), so she should get the woman's own estimate just as though she cut lawns for a living, and accept it if it seemed reasonable.

But the new CR was too emotional to listen and ran off.

Yes, I doubt if a prostitute's own estimate of her monthly earnings would be accurate, but it's something to go by. It's better than nothing. And they may be no more inclined to lie than many other business owners, especially cash-basis ones such as taxi drivers.

Besides, nobody asked her to reveal any illegal activities. As far as I'm concerned, if illegal income is taxable (which it is, as proven by the Al Capone case), then it can be SGA just as much as legal income, if it's high enough.

I see no reason why a prostitute, drug dealer or any other criminal should get a medical decision when somebody making the same income legally can't.

One Potential Problem Could Be Residual Income

The assumptions of the law (and most people, including SSA employees) are if you have a profitable business, you're working in it.

However, some people receive residual income. This is income you receive for work you did earlier.

For example, the only example I ran into was a guy who'd danced in some music videos. He earned royalties for when they were shown on TV and, every so often, the companies sent him a small check.

Some people receive large amounts of residual income. These are generally either creative people or marketing/sales types who enjoy working until they drop.

Let's say you're an Internet marketer receiving $5K per month from your websites, and you've just been diagnosed with a terrible disease and you're too weak to work on your business. But you continue to receive Google Adsense, affiliate and/or CPA commissions and/or product sales income from your sites, because their Google rankings are so strong.

I can understand many CRs would have a hard time thinking you're "disabled" while receiving $5,000 a month, and so would be skeptical of your claim to be no longer contributing toward the business.

You would have to explain that you set the websites up when you were healthier, and specify when you became too ill to continue putting them up. And also explain it's not guaranteed. Google's next major update could wipe you out.

If you get denied on the basis of performing SGA, immediately file an appeal.

It's a hassle but, hey, be glad you've got that five grand coming in whether you're able to work or not.

Impairment Related Work Expenses (IRWE)

After determining your average monthly gross earned income, SSA will need your average medical expenses. That includes what you pay for medicine, for doctor visits and so on.

Frankly, the average American spends very little on these things. Either they're insured and so they pay only the required copays, or they're on Medicaid and getting everything free. So it's rare when IRWE amounts to enough money to take somebody from performing SGA to under SGA.

Your situation may well be different, however. If so, document your expenses. Keep receipts. Know how often you have to buy your prescription medicines and how much they cost.

IRWE can also include things such as buying a wheelchair or paying for extra transportation because you're unable to ride the bus. Think about all the expenses you have because of your medical problem, record and document them.

If your average monthly gross income is under the current SGA level, they'll go ahead and take your claim.

(And keep your wishful thinking in check. Just because your work is below SGA doesn't mean you're disabled. But it does mean you'll get a medical decision.)

If your average monthly gross is over the current SGA level, they'll most likely explain that to you. If you insist on filing a claim anyway, or the office management wants them to take easy denials for the work load units, or the CR wants some fast easy work load units, they'll take the claim and you'll soon get a denial notice in the mail.

They will not take the time to do full documentation of your medical condition and sources, because it's not necessary.

If you are currently working at over SGA, you're not disabled.

In 2012, SGA for disability is $1,010.

(By the way, please note that this is nearly as high as the federal minimum wage of $7.25 per hour times the usual 40 hours per week.)

But I Really Really Really Have X Disease, Pain, Injury Etc

I believe you. But remember that Social Security is a form of "social insurance," not a reward or compensation for your medical problems. It's to help people who cannot perform SGA because of their medical condition. It's not for people who are able to work despite their conditions.

Look around you. Everywhere you go out in the world, you'll see people who are working hard, taking your order at McDonald's, driving trucks, working in a Social Security office...if you could read their medical records, you'd see that many of them have medical problems. They work anyway, or the country would shut down.

I'm Disabled, But I Can't Afford to Stop Working

"Unable" to perform SGA mean you cannot do it even if you want to, even if you have financial necessity (which most people working do have).

What to Do if You are Still Working over SGA

Have a long serious talk with your doctor and, possibly, your employer.

See, it'd be easy to tell you to quit your job and then apply. And many people will tell you to do that. And you might get approved. But you don't have any guarantees. Many get denied.

And if you quit your job for being disabled, you're technically ineligible for unemployment (though many people lie to get unemployment).

So I think it'd be irresponsible of me to give you that advice.

If your medical problems are really so serious, you should be under medical treatment, so ask your doctor about your ability to keep on working the number of hours you are. And find out whether working is aggravating your condition.

And you should have a talk with your employer as well. Can you be given a part-time position that will drop your monthly gross below SGA? Maybe you can be given a light duty job that you can handle for forty hours.

And think long and hard about your body, your condition and your financial future.

Everybody's situation is different. Get the facts on your medical and employment options, and then decide what is best for you.

Do not expect that Social Security will immediately see things your way, or quickly. Plan on it taking months—or even longer—before you begin receiving checks.

If you finally go below SGA either because you leave your job (voluntarily or because of your medical condition) or reduce your hours so you're below SGA, then it's time to apply.

SGA for the Blind (DIB + DWB Only)

All of the above applies for people who have a disability not based on a visual impairment: blindness.

(By the way, this doesn't include normal nearsightedness, farsightedness and astigmatism. Don't bother mentioning those. SSA workers wear glasses just as much as everybody else, so don't ask them to pay you money for that.)

If you do have some severe visual impairment, partial or total blindness, your SGA level is currently (2012) $1,690.

All I can tell you is what I was told in training class many long years ago - the blind have a better lobby than everybody else.

Form 821

If you are still working when you file your disability application, you will need to complete a form SSA-821—if employed—or a Form SSA-820 if self-employed.

They're fairly self-explanatory, especially in light of the information in this chapter.

You can see them here:

http://www.ssa.gov/online/ssa-821.pdf

Michael Schultz

Form 820

http://www.ssa.gov/online/ssa-820.pdf

Date of Onset

For Title 2 Social Security DIB and DWB claims, one of the most critical details is the date of onset.

If you're applying only for SSI, for all practical purposes your date of onset will be the month in which you apply.

For DAC claims, what's important is whether your date of onset is prior to your 22nd birthday.

However, for DIB and DWB it's important to decide in which month exactly you became unable to perform SGA.

Sometimes the date of onset is obvious. You're fine today—until you're in that terrible car accident. Or you suffer a heart attack. Or a stroke. Or you fall off a ladder while painting a house. Or you're shot.

Those are examples of what SSA calls "traumatic onset" disabilities.

One moment you're normal, the next you're not.

If your first stop out of the hospital is the Social Security office to file your claim, obviously you just tell them the date you suffered your traumatic onset.

However, in real life many medical conditions are not so sudden. They build up over time.

When do you become disabled with arthritis? With the first twinge of knee pain you suffer? When you lose your job? When you get a knee replacement?

(You can argue heart attacks and strokes build up over time as well, and I'm sure that's medically true, but you if don't experience any symptoms, your work is not affected.)

Disability Hinges on Work Not Medical Conditions

Therefore, your medical condition can't be disabling until it starts to affect your work.

And where does SSA draw the line regarding work? At SGA.

So it shouldn't be a surprise to learn if you have a chronic condition that's getting worse (arthritis is a good example), SSA will want to know not when you felt your first twinge of pain, or even when you began taking off a day a month because of the pain, but when you had to cut your hours down below the SGA level.

(Actually, the basic history of your problem is still good to put down and explain to provide your medical history, but your date of onset is the month you first became unable to engage in SGA.)

Unsuccessful Work Attempts

Sometimes people suffer from a problem (a heart attack is a good example), go to the hospital, feel recovered, then return to work for a while, then have to stop work (or go below SGA) because of their condition.

What happens then?

It depends.

Examples:

Harry has worked 27 years for the EXY Corporation as a night manager. In May 2010 he suffered a heart attack on the job, went to the hospital, took two months of his sick leave, then returned to his job full time in July 2010.

In March 2011 he suffers a second heart attack and decides to go on disability.

Mary Jane is also working full time for EXY Corporation and has a heart attack in May 2010, then returns to full time work in July 2010.

She also suffers a second heart attack, but in September 2010.

What are their dates of onset? For Harry, it's March 2011. Although he suffered a heart attack in May 2010, he was able to do SGA again for more than six months.

For Mary Jane, it's clearly May 2010. She suffered her second heart attack only two months after returning to work, so that counts as an unsuccessful work attempt.

Remember All SGA Rules

Let's suppose Harry returns to work, but now can do so only part-time. And he has to have more rest breaks than others are allowed. Or he's given special help or treatment or support.

Depending on how much extra help the employer is allowing him, plus how much he has to spend on medicine or other impairment related work expenses, maybe he can make the case that he received a subsidy from his employer and really performed at under SGA.

You Can Allege Any Date of Onset You Want

You can insist on any date of onset you wish, but your state agency worker will follow the rules. If you've done more than 6 months of SGA, it's not an unsuccessful work attempt.

You won't be given a date of onset for a period over 6 months long when you performed SGA.

Yes, you were sick and in pain and so forth, but you continued to earn more than SGA.

Sometimes work fluctuates so much it's difficult to pinpoint these things. You may be asked for your paystubs for that period so Social Security can calculate exactly how much gross wages you earned within each month. Provide them.

The faster you produce such evidence, the more quickly you'll get a decision, and possibly one you like.

If you don't submit your paystubs, you may prevent the CR from calculating months you did go below SGA, which could allow an earlier date of onset.

And if it doesn't, at least you won't have that issue slowing down your payment.

Date of Onset is the Beginning Not the End All, Be All

Social Security takes your date of onset determination very seriously. It can affect how much money you get in a back check because it determines how many months you are owed by the time we make our decision.

It can also affect whether or not you get a DIB check. Sometimes people are right on the borderline of being no longer insured. If SSA cannot find you disabled within the period during which you're insured, you're out of luck so far as DIB is concerned. (Though you may still be eligible for SSI.)

Some DWB applicants are right at the end of their prescribed period.

Don't Wait to Get Medical Treatment

All that is a good reason to get medical treatment for your conditions if you are not already.

It's amazing how many people apply for disability for medical problems they've allegedly suffered for years, and yet have never been treated for them.

SSA will send you to a consultative exam to evaluate your current condition, but it does not have a time machine.

Example:

Jerry comes into the SSA office to file for disability because of arthritis in March 2011. He alleges he became disabled from the arthritis in March 2009. His earnings record verifies he has done no recorded work since 2008.

He alleges not being treated anywhere, so the state agency sends him to a consultative exam. Based on that evidence, his claim is approved.

However, because there is no evidence of impairment prior to him filing his claim, they make his date of onset March 2011.

If Jerry did work five out of the ten years ending March 2011, he'll still get paid DIB benefits based on his earnings, but he will not get back benefits for the past two years.

It would be common for Jerry to be insured in March 2009 but not by March 2011. In that case, he would be denied for DIB but might get SSI.

Why do people do such things as wait two years to file for benefits?

Beats the hell out of me. I don't know why, but I know such situations are far more common than you probably believe. I wish I had a dollar for every Jerry I saw in my 30 years with the agency.

Hazel's story is exactly like Jerry's, except she has been going to her neighborhood clinic every other month for many years.

Therefore, the state agency requests her records and can support a finding her arthritis became disabling in March 2010.

Not as early as Hazel wants, but a year more of back checks than Jerry is going to get.

What if Work is Reduced for Other Reasons?

What if Harry stops work in March 2011 not because of his heart condition, but because the company is going down the tubes and is laying people off?

It appears he retains the ability to continue to do SGA, because that's what he was doing and would still be doing if the company could still afford to pay him.

However, he has the right to file for a DIB claim. If his heart condition is severe enough he may be approved. Maybe it won't be, but he would have no guarantee even if he had suffered the second heart attack.

If you have a severe medical problem and cannot find a job, it doesn't hurt you to file a claim.

You have no guarantees, but you can try, so long as you're honest about it.

Your Disability Journal

When you file for disability, you'll be asked a lot of questions about your medical condition and sources, educational background and work history.

Your educational background should be fairly simple, so long as you remember the highest grade in school you completed, what degrees if any you got, when you got them, and any vocational training you completed. If you're unsure, check those things out.

I'll cover work history in the next chapter.

This chapter suggests before you attempt to file for disability, you take some time to gather all the facts related to your condition and where you're being treated.

Turn off the TV and get away from other noise, someplace where you can relax, think things over carefully and won't be disturbed.

First, list all your medical conditions—both physical and mental.

Just write them all down one at a time.

It's not necessary to have the scientific medical names, but if you do, write them down.

Consult your medical records, your doctor and your list of medicines if that helps.

Write down only conditions affecting you now. When people insisted I put in their gall bladder surgery from twenty years ago, I always figured their current problems must not be very severe. People with currently severe medical problems and limitations don't dwell on history.

But do list everything affecting you now. If you were shot five years ago and the wound is healed but you cannot lift your right hand above your shoulder, that's a current limitation of movement.

For example:

1. Epilepsy

2. Paranoid schizophrenia

3. High blood pressure

4. Arthritis

Then put down how it's affecting you now. Don't write War and Peace, but be specific about how severely it affects you. Use specific numbers if you can. If you do have epilepsy, they'll want to know how often you have a seizure. Once a year is a lot different than once a day.

1. Epilepsy—one to two seizures per week despite taking prescribed medication. No warning.

2. Paranoid schizophrenia—I believe the CIA wants to kill me like it did Osama bin Laden. When I have that feeling, I spend the day hiding under a bush in the park. Average of once a week.

3. High blood pressure—I get dizzy at least once a day despite taking prescribed medications.

4. Arthritis—located in both knees. Moderate to severe pain on a daily basis. Now I cannot run.

When did these conditions begin to affect you? Think back carefully. You probably won't remember an exact day unless you suffered an accident or something, but come up with a reasonable time.

1. First known seizure in 2005

2. November 27, 2010—date family had to call police because I was running around naked in the street threatening people with a knife.

3. Unknown, but first prescribed medication for it in 2009.

4. 2010. Up until 2009 I could still play basketball.

Think carefully about all the places you've been treated. That includes hospitals, clinics and private doctors. Write down as many of the dates as you can remember. Also write down as many of the medical tests you were given as you can.

You may not remember them all. You may have been "out of it," so just do the best you can. Family members can probably help.

You'll be asked for contact details of your medical treatment sources. If they are well-known hospitals and clinics in your local area, your CR and state agency will already know them. If you've been treated by some doctor who still runs their own office, make sure you get that address and telephone number. Also have the precise name—if not address—of any out of town hospitals that won't be familiar to the CR and state agency person.

It's very frustrating to interview someone who says they spent three weeks in "that hospital in Timbucktu New Hampshire" but doesn't know its name. Maybe the CR can find it online, but without the precise name they might find three hospitals in Timbucktu New Hampshire and not know which one you were treated at.

(I once took a claim from a woman treated at The Makati Medical Center in The Philippines. I'm glad they had a website. I'm sure many small rural hospitals around the world do not have a website, so it's up to you to provide the contact info.)

(Once while traveling in a developing country I was panhandled by a woman who not only wanted me to know why her husband could not work, but she showed me his medical records—laminated to keep them in good condition—to prove it. I couldn't help but wish my American claimants were as organized as her.)

Also put down other sources of medical records. Maybe your employer sent you to the "company doctor" last year. Make sure you obtain their name, address and phone number, and dates as close as possible.

If you're being helped by some social service agency, a social worker, a mental health organization—put down all those details. Include if possible the name and phone number of the person working with you. A lot of those places are not centrally organized and have a high turnover rate. Your worker may remember you well, but nobody else will. Your worker may have taken a new job, and without their name nobody can find the records they left behind on you.

Take your time to think carefully, and give it several days. Many times people will remember their main hospital, but forget the counselor they saw only once two years ago, until reminded by writing all this down. If you can remember everything in an hour or two, you didn't get treated enough.

Write down each medication you're taking: the name of it, why you take it and the name of the physician who prescribed it. If you don't know why you're taking it, don't worry about it. Just write it down.

Then think carefully how and when your conditions affected you on the job. Record as much as you can remember when you started feeling pain or tired on the job. Or when you had to take off early or use sick leave to be treated for your condition.

Did your employer have to call an ambulance for you? Give you lighter job duties? Ask a coworker to help you? Adjust your schedule because you could no longer work forty hours a week?

Now think back carefully so you can pinpoint the month your medical condition made you unable to perform SGA. Use your paystubs if necessary.

For many of you, this will be easy. You suffered on the job full-time until something happened and you either quit or were fired and you haven't worked since. The month you stopped working a full-time job will often be your date of onset.

If you stopped working for a time—such as for a heart attack—then returned to work for a time before stopping for good, review the chapter on unsuccessful work attempts.

If you returned to work but stopped in less than 6 months because of your condition you can claim the first date of work stoppage as your date of onset.

If you stopped, then returned for over 6 months you can still claim the first date of work stoppage as your date of onset but you're much less likely to win that date.

(If you're still working full-time you're not disabled.)

If you're still working but doing under SGA, then you must pinpoint the month you went below SGA.

That's assuming you ever did SGA. Some people have never done SGA in their entire lives.

If you've never done SGA, you'll have to think carefully about your medical condition and when you believe it became so bad that you became disabled. Unless that date is very recent, the state agency will want to see good medical records to back up your allegation.

By this point, you should be ready to file the disability application, either completing the 3368 yourself online or giving the information to a CR.

You have at your fingertips:

1. What's wrong with you and how it affects you, and when each condition began

2. Where you've been treated, including dates and medical tests

3. How your conditions affected your work history and the month you became disabled.

Soon after your disability application goes through, you'll probably be mailed a form asking you about your daily activities, the Adult Function Report SSA-3363.

So you may as well get started on that right away:

The form is here:

http://www.ssa.gov/online/ssa-3373.pdf>SSA-3373

Read it over carefully. It may seem overwhelming at first. That's a good reason to get started right away, so you can spend several days thinking over the questions. Do answer all the questions, though not all will apply to your particular disabilities.

If you are alleging a physical disability, it should be obvious the state agency will be most concerned with your daily physical activities.

Start with the time you usually get up in the morning and describe your normal daily activities hour by hour. If you spend a certain period watching TV, put that down. If you visit with your neighbor at 4 PM, put that down.

They'll be concerned with such items as cooking and cleaning. Do you do those things for yourself, do you have help, or does somebody do all that for you?

And have any of those things changed due to your condition? If you used to do all your own house cleaning, but last year stopped because of your arthritis, put that down.

If you used to play basketball twice a week but now can only handle once a month, put that down.

Don't write a full length book, but be comprehensive, truthful and fair to yourself. Don't hold back because some of the questions embarrass you. If you have trouble getting along with people, or concentrating, or paying your bills, put that down. All your answers are protected by the Privacy Act.

If your condition causes you chronic pain, write that down. How often you feel the pain, where, and for how long. And write down what you do to relieve the pain and how well that works.

In many cases the state agency will also need someone who knows you well to fill out a similar form on you, based on what they know about you. If so, you'll also be sent that form, but you can see the Function Report—Adult—Third Party form SSA-3380 here:

http://www.ssa.gov/online/ssa-3380.pdf
I strongly suggest that you continue to keep this disability journal. You may not be approved. You may be denied and want to file an appeal. If so, you will then be asked for all new information regarding your condition since you filed your application.

So continue to record:

1. Dates of all medical treatments

2. Changes in your current medical conditions

3. Onset of new medical conditions

As I mentioned, you'll need that information if you file an appeal.

Your Work History

Now it's time to complete your work journal.

For some people this is very simple (you've worked only one job or none at all). For others it's a major amount of work.

The agency wants to know your work history for the fifteen years prior to your medical conditions beginning to affect you. Depending on your age, you may not have worked that long, so you'll just put down your entire work history.

If you've never worked under paid employment or self-employment, then you can skip this.

List every type of job you had in that period.

That's "type of job," not job.

If you spent five years delivering pizza for Domino's, Pizza Hut, and Papa John's, you can just put down delivering pizzas. You won't be approved or denied because you worked for one fast food chain or another.

Maybe, however, you switched from one type of job to another while working for the same employer. Maybe you went from delivering pizzas for Domino's to store manager where instead of driving around all night, you stayed inside, took orders, made pizzas, cut them, inventoried the store, prepped ingredients and completed final paperwork.

Maybe you've worked for the same corporate employer but you started out as an entry level salesperson and by the time you got sick you were Vice-President of Marketing.

Use common sense. If you were a teacher for twenty years and worked every summer as a swimming pool manager, put down both jobs. If you worked one week as a telemarketer, that's not long enough to be significant.

Unless that week is the only job you've ever had, then put it down.

For every type of work, list your main duties and responsibilities. Think about the physical demands on you. Did you spend more time walking, standing or sitting?

If you were a supervisor, did you spend most of your time as a supervisor or doing actual work?

Put down the technical knowledge you needed and the tools and machinery you used.

Be specific. If you were an MCSE certified network engineer, don't say you "worked with computers." Everybody at a work station thinks they "work with" computers.

If you had to use a blow torch, an x-ray machine or a tractor, put it down.

Think carefully about how much weight you lifted on the job. How much did the heaviest weight you ever lifted. How much weight did you lift frequently?

Of course, on many jobs that won't be significant. If the heaviest weight you lifted was a five pound briefcase, just put that down.

Put down your basic weekly schedule. How many hours per day, how many days per week. On many jobs that's not regular. Other jobs expect you to work irregular overtime as needed. Come up with a fair average.

And put down your rate of pay when you started and when you stopped. You may not remember. If you really were a pizza driver, your tips varied week by week. Put down the best averages you can.

Do that for every type of work from 15 years prior to the beginning of your disability to your last job, or current job if you're still working.

You will need the types of jobs for the form 3368 for the claims interview.

After the state agency gets your claim, it will probably send you a 3369 form asking you about all these details of every job:

http://www.ssa.gov/online/ssa-3369.pdf

Don't stress out about this. Do the best you can. If your jobs are "ordinary" jobs, SSA probably knows what you did better than you remember. I wish I had a dollar for every time somebody told me they worked at a fast food place but wouldn't give me any details and I had to ask questions to prompt them: "Didn't you ever wipe off tables or clean the bathrooms?" (I did when I worked for a restaurant.)

If you had any unusual jobs, be more detailed. If you worked for a circus, in a strip club or planning public events such as conventions, you can't assume SSA and the state agency will know your job, so explain it in as much detail as possible.

And if you ran a business of your own. Some small business owners do everything for themselves, and some hire all their duties out. Be specific about what you did.

The Adult Disability Form – 3368

The 3368 is the basic form for collecting disability information.

http://www.ssa.gov/online/ssa-3368.pdf

It does not apply for SSI children.

Everybody else uses the 3368.

Social Security now has adopted it to an online format, and that's what you'll use if you complete an online disability application.

Section One is basic contact information about you—name, SSN, daytime telephone number and mailing address. And email address.

It includes space for an alternative telephone number. If you have a trustworthy friend or family member, put down their phone number.

SSA also needs to know your languages. If you cannot speak and understand English, or read and understand English, put in your preferred contact language.

Also include any alternative names your medical or vocational records may be in.

Section Two is contact information for anybody who can help you process your claim. Put their name, telephone number, relationship, mailing address and preferred contact language.

If you are helping someone else, put all that information down so SSA can reach you if necessary.

If you're doing it for yourself, just check that box and go on.

Section 3A asks for each separate medical condition that limits your ability to work. Put them all down.

Fill in your weight and height, and whether any of your conditions cause you pain.

(That may sound silly to some of you, but someone with a learning disability doesn't have physical pain from it. You could also have old injuries that affect your physical abilities, but are healed and so no longer cause pain. Anyway, check the answer that applies to you.)

Section 4 is about work activity and is designed to catch unsuccessful work attempts.

It starts out asking about your medical conditions and how they affect you.

It asks for your date of onset, which you have already figured out.

Section 5 covers your Education and Training and is pretty self-explanatory.

SSA needs to know the highest grade of school you finished. If you graduated from high school and stopped, it was grade 12. But if you didn't graduate from high school, you didn't finish grade 12.

If you dropped out of the 11th grade but you have since gotten a GED, and not gone on to college, your highest grade is the GED.

Partial years don't count. If you went to college one and a half years, you finished 13 years of school.

Put in the date you finished your last full year of school.

If you completed college, put in your degree. If you got a postgrad degree, put that in too.

If you went to special ed, put in that information.

And if you completed some type of vocational training, include that in the final question. Whether it was to be a home health aide, auto mechanic or whatever, if you completed the course of training you need to put it down. Write in the type of training and the date you completed it.

The next big section covers your work history.

This starts with the latest type of work you did (on your last job, or your current job if you're still employed). It wants your job title. The type of industry. The date(s) you did this type of work. Your starting and final salary or hourly wage. How many hours a day you worked, how many days a week.

Put down the standard work days and work weeks for you. I know that for some jobs it could vary depending on the business.

All you can do is give the best estimate you can.

The form requires this for every type of work you did in the fifteen years prior to your condition first affecting you.

Notice I keep writing "type of work" rather than job. Many times people will perform the same basic type of work for many different employers.

It makes no difference to your disability case whether you worked for McDonald's or Taco Bell. Basic fast food order taking, cooking and cleaning is much the same for all such jobs.

So is driving a long haul truck or cleaning offices or giving home health care.

The state agency will care what you did on the job, not the name of your employer, so combine all similar jobs together. That can make things a lot simpler.

If you worked only one type of job in the 15 years before becoming disabled, you're asked to supply a lot more detailed information about it.

Then describe your job duties. Put in as much detail as you can about the physical demands made on you by the job, such as how much and how often you had to do heavy lifting. Were you sitting down a lot or standing and walking? Did you do much bending or squatting?

How many hours a day—on average—did you spend walking, standing, sitting, climbing, handling large objects, writing, typing and reaching?

And put down the heaviest weight you ever had to lift, and how much weight you lifted on a frequent basis.

If your job didn't require that kind of physical activity, mark the questions NA for "Not Applicable."

Were you a supervisor? If so, answer how many employees you supervised and how much time you spent being a supervisor instead of a line worker (yelling at employees is being a boss, joining them to wait on customers is being another worker. These roles frequently overlap in some job sites, especially fast food.)

And were you a lead worker, such as a crew leader at McDonald's?

Some people have worked thirty years at the same line of work, but did some part time work on the side. If you spent 30 years as a restaurant chef, the 6 months you once spent as a telemarketer won't mean much.

However, for some people staying on one job for six months is something they've done only once or twice in their whole lives, so those are their most significant jobs.

So my suggestion is to start thinking back over the past 15 years and write down the details of all the main kinds of jobs you've held.

When the 3369 arrives, you'll then be able to complete it quickly, helping to speed up your disability decision.

Section 7 covers your medicines and is fairly self-explanatory. Write down their names, the doctor who prescribed them if they're prescription, and what you take them for.

If they cause you any adverse side-effects, write those down as well. We used to ask for them specifically on the form.

By the way, a side-effect of medicine is something it causes to happen in your body or mind which is NOT why your doctor prescribed the medicine.

I wish I had a dollar for every person who was taking water pills for high blood pressure and said, "It causes me to go to the bathroom a lot."

I always had to point out, "That's not a side-effect. That's what it's supposed to do."

Section 8 just asks you whether you've been treated for your physical or mental medical conditions or whether you have an appointment for treatment.

Some people do check no. Most check yes.

The heart of the 3368 is in Section 8 where you list all your treatment sources. It's fairly self-explanatory, though goes into a lot of detail. If you don't know all the tests you were given, do the best you can.

If you were an inpatient, doctors come and go and you may not know who they were. They should be in the records, so make sure you put down any and every hospitalization.

Section 9 is sort of a catch-all section. Put down any other source of information that may exist on you. This could include organizations that have examined you for a disability pension, life insurance companies, prisons where you were treated, doctors and nurses on your job, social workers—everything else that's not in Section 8.

Don't feel like you have to put something in this section. Most people don't have any such sources. But if you do, put it down here.

Section 10 asks about whether you're getting help from Vocational Rehabilitation, and applies only to people already receiving SSI.

There is a Remarks section if wish to add more information.

You can expand upon your answers if you need to, but it doesn't do you any good to write something the length of an encyclopedia. Nobody has time to read that.

Focus on the specifics of how each of your conditions affects you. If an injury limits how far you can lift your right arm, say so.

If you have epilepsy, put down how often you have seizures. Once a year, once a week, five times a day? I've seen all such allegations, and obviously that makes a difference.

And are you suffering problems despite taking your prescribed medicines and undergoing other treatment?

If your doctor thinks you're not taking the medicine you're prescribed, you can be denied for that reason. The state agency will say you could function well if you'd take your prescribed medications, so take them and go to work. Don't expect the taxpayers to pay you for failing to follow doctor's orders.

Internet Applications

By all means, if you feel comfortable applying for yourself online, do so.

However, the Internet applications I saw were uniformly a mess. People went on and on and on about what was wrong with them. It took longer to edit them than for me to have asked all the questions and written down the people's answers myself in the first place.

Get to the point of each question and stick to it—and put down the facts and nothing but the facts.

And don't repeat the same medical sources ten times. And do fill out all the required spaces.

SSA-827

Your medical sources must obey all the privacy laws, so they cannot release medical records on you to Social Security unless you give permission for them to do so.

Therefore, you are required to sign a medical release.

Here's what it looks like:

http://www.ssa.gov/online/ssa-827.pdf

Yes, it's very detailed and technical, but all you have to do is sign it and fill in your address and telephone number. It does comply with HIPAA and all the latest laws.

It is required. SSA cannot get your medical records without your signature on it, so sign it.

SSI Childhood Medical Claim Forms

In evaluating whether children are disabled, the standard of whether or not they can perform SGA obviously doesn't apply, for only those 16-17 years old can work.

Therefore, the agency looks at whether the child has a medical impairment or combination of impairments that cause "marked and severe functional limitations."

And those impairments and resulting functional limitations must be expected to last a year or longer. Just as with adults, disability for children is for permanent conditions. It's not a temporary disability program.

However, if a child is working, they must not be performing SGA. If a 16 or 17 year old applies and they are working, their earnings are evaluated the same as any adult's, with form SSA-821 for employment and SSA-820 for the self-employed.

As you can figure out, this is rare.

The medical forms for SSI children's disability claims are different than the 3368 for several reasons.

First, children obviously don't usually have important work histories, if any.

Second, because the Supreme Court case made it easier for children to get on SSI than for adults.

Children's claims are even more fully documented than adult claims, if anything.

SSA-3820

First there is the form SSA-3820:

http://www.socialsecurity.gov/online/ssa-3820.pdf

It's somewhat similar to the 3368 in that it does ask all about the child's medical condition and how it affects them.

That begins with basic contact information, including the preferred contact language. They need the child's height and weight.

If the child is enrolled in Medicaid, put in their Medicaid number. Lots of medical records are under that number.

It doesn't delve into date of onset as deeply as Social Security DIB, because for SSI that is going to be the date of application. (It's possible for children to be insured on their own record, but that claim would need a separate 3368.)

However, do put down the date of actual onset to the best of your ability to give the state agency counselor the most accurate picture of your child's condition.

In case of an accident or other injury, the date of onset is the date it happened.

If they've always had asthma or been mentally behind or whatever, put down their date of birth.

Put down the child's medical problems and how they're affected by those problems.

Just as I said in the 3368 section, don't try to write a book. List their impairment(s) and how those condition affect the child.

The Section 3C question never made much sense to me, because "symptom" is such a broad term. If your child has a condition with no symptoms, how would you even know it?

Still, if the child is in pain, certainly put that down.

And of course it also asks about all doctors, hospitals, and clinics where the child has been treated in the past year.

And all medicines they are on. Do the best you can. Maybe you don't know every single thing a doctor or hospital has done. It'll be in the medical records. Put down what you can.

That means ALL hospitalizations and doctor and clinic visits in the past calendar year.

Put down all their current medications, and the tests you know of, to the best of your ability.

And it asks for any other potential sources, such as child care centers, Head Start programs and so on. Think about all the places that know your child, and put them down.

Put down any counselors or therapists they've seen.

The form asks a lot of questions about where the child is currently going to school and where they have been in school in the past year. Put down every school your child attended in the last calendar year. If they were in Special Education or some other type of program related to their disability, make sure you put that down.

If they're too young for school, just check that. Put down any day care centers or preschools they have gone to.

SSA-3881

SSI children's disability or blindness claims also require form SSA-3881.

http://www.ssa.gov/online/ssa-3881.pdf

This form is essentially an expansion of the section of the 3820 that asks about all other (non-school and non-medical) sources of information. It lists a lot more specific possibilities.

Many of the questions won't apply to your child. Don't think your child won't be approved if they haven't been to any of these places.

Although some people think SSA automatically denies all initial claims, this form shows the truth is SSA goes to great lengths to find all possible records on the children who apply for benefits, so all relevant information can be considered.

Social Security must also fill out a development questionnaire on the child. These forms make a lot more sense for some childhood disabilities than others. They make a lot of sense for children filing for being slow learners, but not much for children with asthma. Still, regardless of your child's medical problems, SSA is required to complete the forms.

There are a total of five of these Function Reports:

SSA-3375—for children under 1 year of age

http://www.ssa.gov/online/ssa-3375.pdf

SSA-3376—for children 1-3 years of age

http://www.legisit.com/forms/SSA-3376-BK.pdf

SSA-3377—for children 3-6 years of age

http://www.legisit.com/forms/SSA-3377-BK.pdf

SSA-3378—for children 6-12 years of age

`http://www.legisit.com/forms/SSA-3378-BK.pdf`

SSA-3379—for children 12 to 18 years of age

`http://www.legisit.com/forms/SSA-3379-BK.pdf`

I personally always thought it was crazy to lump six and eleven year olds together, and twelve year olds with seventeen year olds, but I also wouldn't have wanted two or three other separate forms either.

The questions change a lot depending on the child's age.

It's worthwhile giving these questions serious consideration before you go into the local SSA office to file for your child.

I've had many mothers answer them off the tops of their heads and give answers which, considered together, didn't even make sense. For example, mothers would tell me their children couldn't read the alphabet but could read words or sentences. How could that be?

Be accurate, and that should result in consistent answers.

If you don't understand the question, get help from your CR.

Accurate answers can give the state agency counselor a good picture of just how severely your child is affected by their condition. Take your time to fill these forms out. Again, don't write a long novel. But do answer all questions fully and accurately. Keep your answers to the point of the question. Don't repeat your child's disability with every single answer.

Submitting Medical Records

You can expedite your child's claim by submitting records from medical sources with their application.

If your child attends special ed and their school has completed an Individualized Education Plan (IEP) on them within the past calendar year, that can speed things up a lot. I've seen children approved within a week or two just on the basis of the IEP the mother submitted with the application.

If you don't have any records, that's not a problem. Do NOT delay filing a claim to get them. But when you apply, DO list all places where your child has been seen or treated in the past calendar year.

When you file, you are required to sign the same medical release (SSA-827) as adults must do:

http://www.ssa.gov/online/ssa-827.pdf

The Easiest Childhood Disability Claims

If you're filing for a low birth weight baby, that's the easiest application, especially if they're still in an incubator.

Almost no questions on the applications, even the Function Report for babies, applies to them, so the paperwork is easy.

Just take in the hospital records verifying their date of birth, how premature they were, and what they weighed when they were born.

The Consultative Exam (CE)

One of the most important tools the disability counselor uses in deciding whether or not you're disabled is the consultative exam.

That's where they send you out to a doctor who contracts to perform an examination of you. It's something doctors do to make extra cash.

Sending the applicant to a consultative exam is not done for every claim, only when necessary. But it is necessary in most cases.

That's important to remember. The government does not want to pay these doctors unless it needs to.

So if you are sent to a CE, it is necessary. It is required you go.

So if you miss it without notifying your counselor ahead of time and having a very good reason, your claim is denied.

Many Applicants Have Few or No Medical Records

When you apply, SSA asks you where you're being treated: hospitals, clinics and doctors.

Some people have many medical sources, most have at least one or two, but others have none.

SSA cannot make a medical decision without all the required information. The disability state agency attempts to get it first from your medical records. However, if it's not present in your medical records, they must send you to a doctor to get it.

Your Doctor's Job is to Treat You, Not Make a Disability Decision on You

Sometimes people object to attending consultative exams when they have been attending their own doctor or clinic on a regular basis.

Your doctor gets the information they need to make your diagnosis, to prescribe medicine and other treatments for your condition, and then monitor your status.

Maybe they ordered the relevant tests five years ago (too long ago for a disability decision), and have not seen a change since then. SSA wants current test results.

There may well be many cases when SSA requires information for a disability decision your doctor doesn't require to treat you.

Doctors are specialists in their field. If you have many different medical problems, they cannot evaluate all your problems, together with your education and vocational history.

The CE is to Get Additional Information to Make Your Disability Decision

It is NOT to treat you.

If you have not gone out and found a doctor, clinic or hospital for yourself, don't expect Social Security to do that for you.

SSA and the state agencies are not in the business of providing medical treatment or of referring you to any.

If the CE doctor chooses to give you some medical advice, they're being nice. They're not obligated to. So don't expect anything extra.

You're a one-time examination, not a new patient.

You May Need More Than One CE

It's not as common, but sometimes people need more than one consultative exam.

If you want to get approved, go.

The state agency sets up a CE only when it's necessary.

If it's not necessary, they don't do it. The government has to pay the doctor. If they don't have to, they wouldn't. Your state agency worker is evaluated on how quickly they can approve or deny claims. Therefore, they'd prefer not to have to wait for you to go to a CE and to receive the report of their results back from the doctors.

But if they need the additional evidence before making a decision on you, they need it.

So if you're scheduled for a CE, it's not a suggestion, it's a requirement.

What Happens if You Can't Make the CE

My strong suggestion is that if you're scheduled for a CE, go no matter what.

If you have a really good reason for not going (an important appointment scheduled with your very busy doctor, a family funeral to attend), make sure you tell your DDS worker you can't attend it—as soon as possible.

Don't wait until that same day. And certainly don't wait until the day after. By that time they have already heard from the doctor you didn't go, and your claim may already be denied.

If you're not familiar with the address of the CE doctor, go there the day before so you know exactly how to get there, what kind of traffic to expect or what bus to transfer to and when to get off, and you know how to find the exact door you're looking for.

If you get lost the day of the exam so you're late, the doctor may or may not let you in. They're not required to. They have appointments with patients. They're not required to delay seeing a patient because you didn't arrive on time for your appointment.

SSA pays the doctor. Your job is just to show up on time and cooperate with the exam.

Don't Malinger

What happens during the CE varies a lot, depending on your medical condition and what the state agency needs to find out.

Sometimes you're required to take tests.

Knowing that a poor test score may help your claim, you may be tempted to not try as hard as you're capable of. Some people give in to this temptation.

My advice is not to do this. The wording of the law requires you to cooperate with the doctor at the CE, not just show up and go through the motions.

And the doctor is trained at spotting people who are not putting in their full effort. They have a lot more experience at spotting test malingerers than you do at malingering on the test.

If the doctor reports that the tests results are not indicative of your true ability because you failed to cooperate, the state agency worker still does not have the medical information they need to approve you.

And now it's 100% your fault. You failed to cooperate with the exam as you're required to do, so your claim is denied for failure to cooperate and provide necessary information.

What to Do if You Believe the Consultative Exam was Fake

Occasionally I had claimants complain to me the doctor at the CE they were sent to didn't do a good job. They were put through a few simple tests and sent home.

Then the doctor wrote up a report that caused them to be denied, and they didn't feel it was fair.

In some of those cases, I'm sure the doctors performed as they agreed to, but the claimant didn't understand the point of the tests and what the state agency worker needed.

However, doctors can be dishonest too. If a certain doctor is not completing the tests and examinations they agreed to perform on you when they accepted the contract, they are guilty of deceiving and cheating the government, and the government doesn't like that.

If you go to a CE and believe it was not complete, I advise:

1. As soon after as possible, write down everything the doctor did, so you remember as exactly as possible.

2. Call your state agency counselor as quickly as possible and tell them what happened. Tell them what the doctor did. The state agency worker knows what they wanted the doctor to do. If the doctor didn't do all those things, the state agency needs to know— for your claim and for all future CEs in that medical specialty.

Sometimes people don't make these complaints until after they've been denied, and then they just seem to be blaming the CE doctor for their denial.

Make your complaint right away to your state agency counselor, before they make a decision on your case.

Keep Your Mailing Address and Telephone Number Up to Date

One of the biggest reasons people give for missing a scheduled CE is they didn't get the notice (which is often sent by certified mail.)

My advice is to stay at the same address for at least as long as it takes to process your application.

But if you have to move, report it right away. That means calling your CR, calling your state agency worker and putting in a change of address at the Post Office.

If you're one of those people who bounce from pillar to post, have a friend or family member who is stable get your mail for you. And check on your mail at least three times a week.

It does no good to get a notice if you don't read it because you're too busy running the streets.

If you're in an area where mail gets stolen (especially if the return address is a government agency), get a Post Office box or have your mail go to a trusted friend or family member in a better neighborhood.

Pay attention to your mail every day, and keep it out of the hands of young children.

There's no doubt in my mind many (probably the great majority) of the people who told me they didn't get a particular notice or letter from SSA did have the letter placed in their mailbox, but didn't pay attention to it, or children in the household played with it without any adult intervention.

If you have an outside mailbox mail can be stolen from, watch for your mail carrier and get the mail right away.

If you have a slot in the front door, that protects the mail from strangers, but leaves it vulnerable to small children and pets, so pick it up right away.

And look at it.

If it's from Social Security, you know it's important, so open it right away.

Do everything in your power to make sure you get your mail from SSA. You can't control what Post Office employees lose, but you can control what you lose.

CE notices are generally sent by certified mail.

If you get a green receipt in the mail notifying you of certified mail, go to the Post Office and claim it right away. It's amazing how often people refuse to do this, and then whine about how they didn't get the notice. They didn't get the notice because they failed to go to the Post Office to get it.

Sometimes the certified letter is received at the house. The Post Office sends it back to SSA with a signature. Who knows who signed? A young teenager? A neighbor? A home health aide?

If you allow anybody to go to the front door to get your mail for you, you better make sure they give you any certified mail they sign for.

It's important to emphasize. If you need a CE, you must attend it or you'll be denied.

It's your responsibility both to provide an accurate mailing address—and telephone number if possible—and to check on your mail on a frequent, regular basis.

You probably don't even realize how many people don't get their mail daily, but failure to attend consultative exams is one of the most common single reasons people are denied for disability.

Title 2 Disability Benefits

The main Title 2 Social Security disability benefit is for wage earners. That is, people who worked enough to be insured. And the worker is either expected to die within a year or will be unable to perform SGA for at least a year.

This is covered extensively in this book. Most everything I wrote about applying for disability benefits as an adult applies to this.

Disabled Widow(er) Benefits

You must be found disabled.

Other requirements for DWB:

You're at least age 50 but below age 60.

You prove you were married to the deceased wage earner.

The deceased wage earner must have been insured.

Generally, your disability must have begun within 7 years of the wage earner's death.

If you remarry before the age of 60, you are no longer eligible for DWB on the prior spouse's record. However, you are allowed to remarry after age 60.

Disabled Adult Child (DAC)

Social Security was designed to help the dependents of wage earners who are disabled, retired or deceased.

That generally includes spouses and minor children.

However, some children are disabled and so unable to support themselves even after they are no longer minors.

Therefore, if you or someone you care for is the child of a disabled, retired or deceased wage earner, they have never married, and they became disabled prior to age 22, they should apply.

Most such children are disabled prior to age 18 and SSA takes their application at age 18. However, of course it's possible for someone to be not disabled at the age of 18 but become disabled prior to age 22.

The definition for disabled is the same as for insured workers.

However, the law takes the position if someone is mature enough to get married, they're no longer entitled to the legal benefits of being labeled a "child."

Therefore, someone who has married is not eligible for DAC benefits. DAC beneficiaries who get married are supposed to report, because that terminates their eligibility for DAC benefits.

Retirement and Survivors (RSI) Title 2 Benefits

The main one is retirement (RIB). That's mainly what I discuss in this book in this area.

The following benefits revolve around the retirement or disability of a wage earner, or the death of a wage earner.

There's not much to say except if you believe you're eligible, go to Social Security with the required proofs. You'll need marriage certificates, divorce decrees, birth certificates of children and death certificates.

These benefits are mainly about you supplying SSA with the proofs they need.

My focus in this book is on getting retirement, disability, Medicare and SSI.

Spouse's Benefits

You must be the spouse of a wage earner receiving either retirement or disability benefits.

You must have been married to the wage earner at least 1 year prior to the day they file an application for benefits.

Be the natural mother or father of the wage earner's biological son or daughter

You must not be entitled to retirement or disability benefits on your own record which equal or exceed one-half of the spouse's amount. (If you are, SSA will simply pay you what you're eligible for on your own record.)

Be at least 62 years old OR have a child of the wage earner in your care under age 16 or disabled.

Divorced Spouse

To get as a divorced spouse you must have been married to a wage earner receiving retirement or disability for at least 10 years.

You must be age 62.

You must not be entitled to retirement or disability benefits on your own record which equal or exceed one-half of the spouse's amount. (If you are, SSA will simply pay you what you're eligible for on your own record.)

You must not be married.

Independently Entitled Divorced Spouse

Be the divorced spouse of a fully insured wage earner who is at least age 62

Be divorced from the wage earner for at least 2 years.

Meet the other requirements for Divorced Spouse

Child Benefits

Be the minor child of a wage earner receiving retirement or disability benefits, or who is deceased and insured.

Widow(er) Benefits

You must be the widow(er) of a wage earner who was insured at their time of death.

You were married to the wage earner at least 9 months prior to their date of death.

You must not have caused the wage earner's death (Sounds funny when you first read it, but it's not when you consider how many husband and wives do kill their spouses. The government does not want a murderer collecting benefits created by their victim's death.)

You are at least 60 years old.

You're currently unmarried.

Not be entitled to retirement benefits on your own record which equals or exceeds the deceased spouse's.

Surviving Divorced Spouse

You must be the surviving divorced spouse of a wage earner who died insured.

You must be at least 60 years old.

You must be unmarried.

Not be entitled to retirement benefits on your own record which equals or exceeds the deceased spouse's.

Mother/Father's Benefits

You must be the widow(er) of a deceased wage earner who is insured.

You must not be married.

You're not entitled to widow(er) benefits.

You must not be entitled to retirement benefit that equal or exceed the Mother/Father benefit

You must have in your custody and care of a child of the deceased wage earner.

You must not have caused the wage earner's death (Again—it sounds funny when you first read it, but it's not when you consider how many husband and wives do kill their spouses. The government does not want a murderer collecting benefits created by their victim's death.)

Parents Benefits

You must be the parent of a wage earner who was insured when they died.

You're at least 62 years old.

You're not entitled to retirement that equal or exceeds the wage earner's.

You were not married after the wage earner's death.

You were getting at least one-half support from the wage earner.

You must not have caused the wage earner's death.

All of these types of benefits are for dependents of the wage earner.

First of all, somebody must have worked long enough to be fully insured.

Then the wage earner must themselves be retired, disabled or dead.

Then their spouse or children can draw, depending on the details.

I don't know the statistics kept by the agency, but I suspect dependent spousal benefits are going way down. That's because although their names are now gender-neutral, they started out as being mostly for wives, on the assumption the wife of the wage earners stayed at home taking care of the kids while he worked.

We live in a different social order today. Most wives are out earning money on their own records, and so when they get old enough or disabled, will simply draw on their own records.

Still, if you believe you may fit one of the above categories, get all your relationship proofs together and take them to your local Social Security office.

They will also need the wage earner's Social Security number.

Government Pension Offset

One major reason for the existence of spouses who have not paid as much into Social Security as their partner is not only many of these spouses have been traditional housewives, but many of them worked for organizations where the employees aren't covered by Social Security.

This includes federal employees hired before 1984 who didn't switch to FERS, Post Office employees, teachers, police, fire fighters and other state and local employees.

These people are all under their own separate pension systems.

There had been political pressure to "do something" about spouses who collect their own pensions (without ever paying into Social Security) and who also collect Social Security spousal benefits based on what their spouses paid into Social Security.

So Social Security began "offsetting" the Social Security spousal checks of spouses collecting their own pensions for noncovered (that is, work where Social Security FICA taxes was not taken out) employment.

This is known as Government Pension Offset (GPO).

Therefore, if you have (or are) the spouse of someone who is applying for Social Security retirement or disability on their own record, if you meet the main requirements for spousal benefits you'll be asked whether you are receiving a pension for noncovered work.

If you are, SSA will need to verify the monthly amount, so take your most recent benefit letter or other verification into the local office with you.

They'll also need the information on form SSA-3885, Government Pension Questionnaire.

http://www.ssa.gov/online/ssa-3885.pdf

But in the SSA office the CR will record the information on their computer screen.

GPO does not apply to pensions from private companies or unions (because the employees paid into the system with FICA taxes) or from foreign government employment (because Social Security and FICA don't apply to any employment outside the U.S. anyway.)

The spousal Social Security benefit check is cut by 2/3 of the gross amount of their noncovered government pension.

Examples:

Joe is filing for RIB. His wife Jane is a retired schoolteacher who collects $2,100 per month from the state of Illinois. Based on what Joe paid into Social Security, Jane's wife's benefits would be $850.

2/3 of $2,100 = $1,400

$1,400 - $850 = $0

Jane is not due any spousal Social Security benefit, because 2/3 of her pension is higher than the Social Security monthly benefit amount.

This is called total GPO, because Jane is due no SSA wife's check.

Same as above, only Joe earned a lot more money, so Jane's wife's benefits would be $1677.

2/3 of $2,100 = $1,400

$1,677 - $1,400 = $277

Jane gets a monthly check from SSA for $277.

That's Partial GPO, because Jane's pension check just partially offset her wife's benefits.

If Your Spouse is Not a U.S. Citizen or Resident

There is a residence requirement for spouses as well.

They must have resided in the United States for at least five years and been your spouse for at least five years.

Therefore, if you retired to Mexico, Costa Rica, Thailand or some other country as an unmarried person, but you've met someone local you want to marry, they cannot get spousal benefits on your record unless they move to the U.S. and live there, married to you, for five years.

If You Have a Child Outside the U.S.

If you have a child born outside the United States, they are eligible for child's benefits on your record for the first six months they are outside the United States.

If you and the child continue to live outside the U.S., the child's benefits are suspended.

To receive child's benefits again, the child must live in the U.S. for five years, or you must move back to the U.S. and die there (not outside the U.S.)

Fraud and Similar Fault

One role of the Claims Representative and state agency disability examiner jobs is to detect fraud and refer possible cases of it for additional investigation and possible prosecution.

Fraud is the intentional misrepresentation of information and evidence to qualify for benefits or more benefits than you're not truthfully entitled to.

I strongly suggest you decide to remain honest. You'll be able to sleep better at night knowing your quest for disability or retirement checks won't end in a jail term or huge fine.

One thing to keep in mind is even though SSA workers are government employees, they are not stupid. One characteristic of many fraud referrals I made was the people almost inevitably thought they were smarter than they were, or we were too stupid to detect them.

(If you were receiving disability would you go on TV shows—including big name nationally syndicated talk shows—as a comedian? Somebody did just that. I guess he thought SSA workers are put into a box at night, and don't watch TV like everybody else.)

SSA and DDS workers have seen many cases. It doesn't take long before you know what is "normal," and what sounds your alarm bells.

Everybody Spins

I've had people look at me and tell me they're in "agony all the time." Yet they were not screaming throughout the interview, so obviously they were not telling me the literal truth.

But they did have a disease or injury that caused them a lot of pain. They know the pain goes up and down, but it sounds better when you're applying for disability to say it's "constant."

That is spin, not fraud.

They might then go to a job interview and assure the prospective employer the pain wouldn't keep them from performing their job duties. I'm sure some of them did just that.

The pain is the pain, but how we describe it to others depends on what we want from them.

Everybody Also Exaggerates for Effect

We all tend to exaggerate when we talk about ourselves, if only for emphasis. That's okay with friends and family.

But when you go to your local SSA office or speak to them on the phone, I advise you to be very precise in what you say.

Tell the truth, the whole truth and nothing but the truth.

Unfortunately, many people are not used to being precise in their thinking and speaking.

Besides, to get disability you don't have to be in horrible agony every second of your life. You do have to have medical records that document your illness or injury and its severity.

But if you walk into the office wearing dark glasses holding your mother's arm and allege total blindness, and SSA later discovers you're driving a taxi, they'll go after you. (A frightening number of taxi drivers have real visual impairments (though not total blindness), but drive anyway.)

Retirement Fraud is Most Difficult

That's because your birth certificate and allegations on prior Social Security card applications are what they are.

If you've been alleging since you were 16 you were born in 1955, but now you claim it was really 1947, you better have a birth certificate. If you've altered it, it will most likely be apparent.

(OK, maybe not if you're a professional forger. But if you are, you'd be a lot smarter forging something worth a lot more money than the average SSA check.)

Also, it will still be double-checked with the issuing vital statistics branch of that state government, so if you're lying you'll still be caught.

Disability Fraud

This is probably the biggest area of abuse in the Social Security system.

Some types of conditions are so bad they're not faked. (I never had anybody tell me they had stage 4 cancer, unless they really did).

Others are simply Heaven for scammers. Depression. Back problems. For SSI children, ADHD.

I'm not saying everybody with one of those conditions is a scammer, just those conditions are more easily abused.

If you really have such a condition or conditions, I strongly suggest you get as much medical treatment for it as possible, not just to benefit from the treatment, but also to document your problems and severity with as much credibility as possible.

((Once I took a claim from a young man who thought government checks should be easy to get applied for SSI disability (he hadn't worked enough to be insured for DIB) because of his bad back. But he told me that he passed the time playing basketball, and had no treatment records. He didn't go to jail, but he didn't get a government check either.))

Basic Fraud Procedures

If you do something that makes a CR refer you for fraud, they will write up a referral to the Office of Inspector General (OIG) requesting an investigation by a trained agent. They'll describe the facts and evidence.

A lot depends on the seriousness of the allegations, whether you've misrepresented something or merely "forgot" to tell SSA something. And whether you've presented fake evidence or altered documents.

(I believe by the time a case gets in front of a jury, nobody cares what you did or did not tell a CR, but physical evidence of intent to deceive could send you to jail.)

The agents investigate all the facts, and check you out. At some point they may interview you. I'm not sure of all their protocols. If SSA asks you in for an interview related to fraud, you'll be read your rights.

If OIG believes your case has merit, they give it to the local federal prosecuting attorney who has to decide whether to take you to court or not. If so, you're arrested and things proceed from there.

If you're convicted, part of your sentence can include fines and restitution ordered by the court.

Frankly, only a relative few cases go to court.

But that doesn't mean you're free and clear.

I once referred a man for fraud who was out of prison on probation. He didn't go to jail for SSA fraud, but returned to prison for violating probation.

(He's also another example of people who are so greedy for "free" government checks they ruin their lives. He deliberately misrepresented his work, and then quit the job thinking that would protect him.

It was the best job he'd ever had (most of his adult life had been spent in jail). If he'd simply kept his job and agreed to repay his overpayment (we would have approved a payment plan he could afford), I would not have referred him for fraud. But he was too smart for that...

People Prosecuting Attorneys LOVE to Send to Jail...

You may have heard jokes about people who are receiving SSA checks for Grandma who's living with them. When Grandma finally dies, they conceal her death and continue cashing her checks.

Unfortunately, there are many real life examples of this.

OIG investigators are experienced at digging up basements and backyards.

Every so often, SSA district managers must verify the continued existence of the elderly recipients in their district. If they can't see Grandma in person, alive in her bed upstairs, they'll send out the investigators.

So you'll get caught eventually.

Federal prosecutors are often reluctant to try to convict elderly and disabled people. But sending you to jail for hiding Grandma's body and continuing to cash her checks—that's great publicity for them. Don't expect any sympathy.

Similar Fault

What about (many) people who are never prosecuted? Do they just walk?

In terms of jail, yes. In terms of money, no.

Once SSA documents you've gone out of your way to receive benefits incorrectly, SSA can charge you with an overpayment for the entire period no matter how long.

(Normally, they're limited to going back only two years.)

They can also charge you with penalties.

Plus, if you remain eligible for SSI, they can withhold 100% of your check to repay your overpayment.

What does SSA expect you to live on? Think about that if you're ever tempted to defraud Social Security.

While most of the fraud I saw came from working my job, SSA also gets reports of fraud from ordinary people.

People who defraud SSA also seem to be the kind of people who are hated by their neighbors, friends, family members, ex-spouses and ex-boy and ex-girlfriends.

Who are then motivated to get revenge by reporting the fraud to SSA.

If you know of someone who, you believe (bear in mind you don't have all the facts at your disposal), may be committing SSA fraud, report it here:

http://www.ssa.gov/oig/hotline/index.htm

1-800-269-0271 from 10:00 a.m. to 4:00 p.m. E.S.T.

TTY: 1-866-501-2101

At SSA, Consistency is Your Best Friend

The most well-known and important book on persuasion—INFLUENCE: The Art of Persuasion by Robert Cialdini—lists consistency as one of the six principles of persuasion.

I'd have to say, after my 30 years with SSA, for applying for benefits it's the most important element.

To be fair, I'm not saying if your medical records don't establish your condition is severe enough to meet the listings, being consistent will force SSA to find you're disabled anyway. It won't force SSA to pay you retirement benefits if you're under age 62.

But in many cases it can help you, because many cases center around just how severe your medical condition is. That is, how much it affects your life and activities, especially your ability to work.

Back in the Days of Date of Birth Determinations

Back when I began working for SSA, a major work load of CRs was making date of birth determinations.

People would come in saying they were age 62 but not have a birth certificate, and had been unable to get one from the state vital statistics department.

Good record keeping of vital statistics in the United States was not universal for people born in the early 20th century, especially people born in rural areas, at home with midwives, and in the South.

Therefore, we had to get as much additional documentation as possible, though nothing is as good as a birth certificate or a detailed and early baptismal record.

So we'd look at family Bibles, children's birth certificates, life insurance policies, military discharge papers, marriage certificates, and anything else people could bring in. Then we'd have to evaluate the evidence and reach the best conclusion we could.

The more you used the date of birth you now want to file a retirement claim on THROUGHOUT your life, the easier it was to determine it was accurate.

Sometimes people did have logical explanations for inconsistencies. Men would make themselves older than they were to join the Army. Women would make themselves older than they were to get married. Both would make themselves older than they were to get a job.

And some women would make themselves younger when they got married late in life.

I remember talking to one woman who had told her husband they were the same age, but she was actually 25 years older than him. I had to be careful, because he was present during the interview and the Privacy Act means I could not reveal her true age to him, so I had to talk around it.

The World Is Stricter Now

Many women use a husband/ex's last name when applying for benefits on his record, but their maiden name on their job. And their current boyfriend's last name on their apartment lease.

Many women tell the child's school the child's last name is her maiden name, but tell Social Security the child's last name is the last name of the man they're alleging is the child's father.

Many women get married and don't change their names on their Social Security cards right away, then wonder why the couple's tax refund is held up by the IRS because her Social Security Number doesn't match up.

In older times—I (and many of you) will recall—when paperwork was done on you, you were believed. At least, it was not cross-checked. It was not practical for SSA, the IRS, local governments, life insurance companies, banks, vital statistic record keeping departments or anyone else to double check details. I don't recall ever manipulating my personal information, but I now realize that I could have—and many people did (and still do).

However, the massive computerization of the world is forcing consistency.

Maybe you didn't even notice. For instance, if you were born late in the 1970s or later, when your parents applied for a Social Security number for you, they were required to show SSA your birth certificate. That was recorded.

Maybe you have since received replacement Social Security cards. You had to show SSA some ID, but the basic information regarding your date of birth, place of birth and so on was automatically carried over from one application—SS-5 form—to the next. You were not given the opportunity to give SSA a false date of birth.

If you ever file for DIB, SSA will use that date of birth. The same when you file for RIB.

You won't ever have to prove your date of birth to Social Security because your parents did it for you while you were a baby.

When us old farts got Social Security cards, SSA just accepted the allegations of our date of birth. It remains unproven. However, if you have remained consistent and used the same date of birth on Social Security replacement cards, SSA is going to accept this allegation for your RIB claim. I believe it will be automatic if you file online—which the agency is pushing because it does not have nearly enough staff to take in-person RIB claims and request birth certificates for the gazillions of baby boomers who are going to retire in the next 20 years.

If you have been inconsistent and used different dates of birth, your claim will take longer because the agency will have to check your birth records.

(If you know you've been inconsistent, I strongly suggest your send for a certified copy of your birth certificate months before you actually apply for RIB.)

Consistency is Important in DIB Cases as Well

Example: Derek files for DIB alleging he has depression and high blood pressure. He has no medical treatment records, so he is sent to two consulting physicians. One of them has to evaluate his claim of high blood pressure and the other is a psychiatrist.

However, virtually all medical exams ask you a broad range of questions. When the psychiatrist asks him if he has any physical problems, he says, "No."

When the internal medical MD asks him what his general mood is like, he says, "Great."

They don't follow up, because that's outside their areas of specialization. But the state agency worker will read the reports from both doctors, look at these inconsistent allegations and very likely determine Derek needs to look for a job.

You Must First of All Remain Consistent With the Facts

If you use 1958 as a date of birth throughout your life but your birth certificate shows 1959, obviously SSA will use the 1959 date.

Alleging constant chest pains won't help you if an EKG shows your heart is normal.

You Should Also Keep the Facts Consistent With Your Allegations

For example, if you tell us your back pain prevents you from performing normal physical activities, don't go for very long walks, vacuum the inside of your automobile at a car wash (getting on your hands and knees to stretch that nozzle all the way under your seat), or lift several cases of soda cans at a 7-Eleven and load them into your SUV.

(All real cases.)

This is a fairly common scenario:

A disabled woman applies for SSI saying she is separated from her husband. She gets approved and starts receiving benefits.

Years later that woman comes into SSA. Her husband died recently, and she wants the $255 lump sum death benefit. She tells the CR she's been living with him since 20XX (a date going back years), so she gets her $255.

However, SSI is a needs based income. When you're on SSI and living with your spouse, your spouse's income and resources affect your payment amount.

Sometimes the date she gives is prior to her claim for SSI, indicating she lied on her SSI application.

Sometimes the date she gives is subsequent to her claim for SSI, indicating she and the husband really were separated when she filed for SSI, later got back together, but she failed to report this material change as she was required to do.

Either way, a CR will then check on the husband's income for that period, often finding wages, Social Security, unemployment or other types of income.

The woman eventually gets a humongous SSI overpayment letter.

It's Amazing How Many People Tells Lies that Delay Their Checks

I wish I had a dollar for every time I've asked someone during an initial application whether they owned something, they said yes, but after lots of time, it turns out they didn't.

This most often involved life insurance policies. Somebody would tell me they owned such and such life insurance policy. They could give only sketchy details, but that was normal.

So I had to request to see the policy, then all of a sudden there'd be drama about how it was at their sister's house and she wouldn't let them have it or some other bizarre story.

But it was too late. They'd already attested to ownership of that policy, so I had to see it.

After weeks of follow ups and telephone calls from them telling me how much they needed their money but them failing to provide the proof I needed to pay them, they'd send in a letter from the insurance company showing their policy had been cancelled for nonpayment of premiums – 10 years ago!

Or it turned out they'd once talked to an agent but never really taken out a policy.

Or it was a fire insurance policy, not life insurance.

Property Verification is Often a Problem Too

One time a man told me he owned some property. I checked the records and, according to the assessor's office, he did own it, and its tax-assessed value put him over the SSI resources limit, meaning he was not eligible.

Eventually he came in with a quit claim deed indicating he had signed away ownership of the property EIGHT YEARS AGO. But nobody had bothered to inform the tax assessor.

And to me he alleged he still owned it.

Just as you should not tell lies to conceal things, you also should not tell lies that you own property you gave away eight years ago.

No CR wants to delay paying you your money, because the faster claims are paid, the better they look.

However, they must also remain accurate. If you allege owning life insurance policies, properties or other such resources, they must be verified.

Making things up hurts your CR and hurts you, so know what you own. Tell the truth about that.

Tell the CR what you own, but nothing you don't own. That's fair enough.

Why do people do these kinds of things?

I have no idea. I hope as someone motivated to read this book, you've got your life (and mind) in better order.

Consistency in Lying Invites a Fraud Referral

So far, however, I've assumed the truth is to your advantage.

If you are deliberately lying to Social Security, to continue lying can actually make things worse in the end.

For example: in the case of the women who fail to report living with a husband, if they have continued that lie on SSI Redetermination Forms, and the CR decides to refer them for fraud, every Redetermination Form will be a "count" or separate violation, or at the least will be used to prove an intentional pattern of behavior meant to deceive Social Security.

According to Ralph Waldo Emerson, Inconsistency is the hobgoblin of little minds.

However, if you wish to receive the most benefits you're eligible for, as quickly as possible, you'd be wise to give the "little minds" at SSA 100% consistency.

Appeals

Contrary to rumor, SSA does NOT deny all initial claims. If that were true, everybody would get a denial notice within a week. Why would SSA even bother to request your medical records and send you to a doctor's exam?

However, that doesn't mean everybody who applies is approved. More than half are denied.

That's not because SSA is a big blue meanie. It's partly because lots of applications deserve to be denied.

Other applications are not pursued by the applicants. They don't provide requested evidence and don't go to consultative exams. Many of these people would get approved if they cooperated with the claims process, but they don't, so their claims are denied.

There are cases where there's simply disagreement over the issue of disability. Many cases are not clear-cut and obvious.

You may believe your case is clear-cut and obvious. If that's true, you won't need to file an appeal.

But the vast majority of disability applicants are not as bad off as they believe. That doesn't mean they're in great health. It just means that they're not the unhealthiest, unluckiest person in the world even though they want SSA to believe that.

I don't know who you are, and I may not want to trade places with you (I'm in reasonable good health), but if you're able to read this, I've met many people who are in worse shape than you.

You Have the Right to File an Appeal

However, Congress always knew there'd be disagreements over the issue of disability. That's why they established the appeals process.

If you are denied for an application for benefits, you have the right to file an appeal to get a second opinion.

On disability claims, the first level of appeal in most of the United States is the reconsideration.

Your case goes back to the state agency. It will go to a state agency worker who did NOT work on your initial claim.

You have 60 days from the date of the initial claims denial letter to file a reconsideration form SSA-561.

http://www.ssa.gov/online/ssa-561.pdf

But why wait?

SSA will even extend that 60 days if you can come up with a good story about why you couldn't come in within 60 days.

But let's face it, if you really care about your claim, it shouldn't take more than one business day to get to your nearest field office.

If you believe you're disabled and you need the money, barring health emergencies, doctor appointments and bad weather (none of which last 60 days), you should get to your local SSA office.

Do NOT Wait for Anything

Do NOT wait for advice from your doctor, for medical records, to see a lawyer or to talk it over with all your friends and family.

If you disagree with the decision, file the appeal right away.

You can do so by mail, but that wastes time, because your local SSA office will still have to contact you to complete the medical update form and get a new medical authorization form signed.

The sooner you get it started, the sooner you'll get your second decision.

If you're following my advice to keep a medical diary, bring that with you. The CR will want to update your medical background, so you'll want to be able to answer all their questions.

The SSA-3441 Reconsideration Medical Form

You can see it here:

http://www.ssa.gov/online/ssa-3441.pdf

The CR will ask you all of those questions about changes in your medical condition since you filed your initial claim.

They do NOT want a repeat of your initial disability allegations. They're interested in changes since you applied.

If your condition is worse or better.

Different medicines, additional medical treatment, hospitalizations, and so on.

If you've worked since your initial claim, be prepared to answer questions about that on a form SSA-821 or SSA-820, which I cover in Chapter 8 on SGA. It'd best to bring in all paystubs you've received since your initial application.

If your initial claim was denied because you failed to go to a consultative exam, another one will be set up for you.

Make sure you keep the appointment.

If you failed to provide some kind of medical evidence or to complete a form—do what you failed to do.

If you repeat your errors of the initial claim you'll get the same decision. You're wasting your own and everybody else's time.

The state agency worker will get all the information they need to make another, current decision on your case. Then they will make it.

It may be the same, it may be different.

If you're disabled but you originally were denied because you failed to attend your consultative exam and this time you attend it, then the state agency worker will this time have the facts.

Maybe something else will have changed. Maybe you had to be hospitalized since your initial claim and that indicates your condition has gone downhill.

Sometimes the state agency counselors simply disagree with each other. The second one will approve you even though the first one didn't. I've seen that happen in a short time, but don't count on it.

Just as every case is different, so every reconsideration is different.

However, many times the reconsideration decision will also be a denial.

What then?

You have 60 days to take the next steps, which is a hearing.

Do NOT Wait to File a Hearing

I give the same advice here—in spades!

Apply for your hearing IMMEDIATELY upon receiving a reconsideration notice you disagree with.

The form is SSA-501:

http://www.ssa.gov/online/ha-501.pdf

Hearings are much more complicated than reconsiderations, and take MUCH longer.

You really really really want to get your request for a hearing into SSA as soon as humanly possible.

Do not wait for a lawyer, your doctor, an auspicious astrological day or anything else. Go into your SSA field office the very next business day.

The medical update form will be used to find out if there have been any changes since you filed for your reconsideration.

They now use the HA-4631 Claimant's Recent Medical Treatment:

http://www.ssa.gov/online/HA-4631.pdf

And the HA-4632 Claimant's Medications:

http://www.ssa.gov/online/HA-4632.pdf

If you've worked since you filed for the reconsideration, they'll also get HA-4632 Claimant's Work Background:

http://www.ssa.gov/online/HA-4633.pdf

And they'll want another SSA-827 Medical Authorization:

http://www.ssa.gov/online/ssa-827.pdf

The field office will then ship your hearing request to the Hearing and Appeals Office.

It is now a legal matter. Eventually the hearings office will schedule a hearing for you with an Administrative Law Judge (ALJ).

They have the best jobs in SSA. They get paid an outrageous amount of money. They work only as many cases as they choose, and take as long as they choose. And can make any decision they choose.

They are supposed to find people disabled within the Social Security law, but they have the right to be far more generous in interpreting the law than do state agency workers, who must follow strict guidelines.

The hearings office may ask you to do other things as well. They may request you go to another consultative exam. They may send you more forms to complete.

Do what they ask, that's my advice. And the sooner the better. The process takes long enough as it is. Don't you make it any longer than necessary. Whatever they want, give it to them.

Take the time to do a good job, but don't delay it.

That applies especially to the hearing.

Once you get the notice of hearing, go to that office the next day so you know how to get there. So you know all the streets to take and where you can park. Or all the bus transfers you have to make.

If you fail to show up for your hearing, it will be dismissed.

Go to the hearing.

If you're lucky, you'll get a hearing decision within one year of requesting it. Some extreme cases are moved forward very quickly. Other cases take longer. If your lawyer files a lot of motions to delay the hearing, it could take up to two years for your decision.

If you fail to show up on time for your hearing, you will have royally screwed yourself.

Can I say it any plainer?

So everything I said earlier about having a permanent mailing address, reporting changes to SSA, the Hearings Office and the Post Office immediately, checking on your mail every two days, and so on—applies to hearings even more so.

That's especially true even though there will be many long months when you do not hear from the Hearings Office and you think they've forgotten you.

You're not their first or their only hearing, so they can delay your case, but you're not forgotten forever.

Social Security and SSI Offset

SSI is based on income received in that calendar month.

Therefore, many years ago, when somebody was approved at the hearings level for both Social Security and SSI, their SSI back check was calculated using whatever income they actually received.

One kind of income they did not receive in those months was Social Security. Both types of benefits were waiting for the hearing decision.

On the surface, that makes sense.

But the consequence of that was when they were found disabled by a hearing decision and SSI and Social Security had to be back checks going back one, two or even more years, they received a FULL Social Security back check and a FULL SSI back check.

However, somebody high up in the government finally figured out what every Social Security claims representative already knew, and that this arrangement was unfair to the taxpayers.

Think about it.

If the claims of these people had been approved right away, they would receive Social Security right away, and SSI would then use their Social Security income to compute their SSI checks.

But because the Social Security checks were delayed, they got both Social Security and SSI in full.

So the government passed a law to have the back checks "offset" against each other. They're netted out so that people get back payments that total only what they would have received had they been paid correctly all along.

This does create some delay in the payment process. The SSI review has to be completed before Social Security can release their back check, so the Social Security back check can be reduced by the SSI amount.

And it gets even more complicated because the lawyers got involved. Now, before back money is released to the claimant, the lawyer's 25% has to be calculated and paid to them.

(Too many people were stiffing their lawyers, and of course Congress sympathized with the poor lawyers.)

Therefore, if you are approved for any kind of back payment of both Social Security and SSI, my advice is to cooperate as quickly as possible. Go into Social Security to complete the SSI review immediately. If they need evidence, provide it immediately.

Take with you:

All life insurance policies

All bank statements from the first day of the month you applied in to the present month for you, your spouse, or the parents of a child

All paystubs for you, your spouse, or the parents of a child

If you're renting, your rent receipt

If you live with someone else and buy food separately or pay any money on the bills, bring the householder with you (If you get food and shelter and don't pay on the bills, there's no need. SSA will accept your word that you're in a living arrangement B.)

Proof of any other income you've received from month of application to date

Proof of any other resources you've owned from month of application to date

If you don't apply for SSI, this section doesn't apply to you.

(Except if you have a lawyer, your back Social Security will not be released to you until the lawyer's amount is calculated and paid. However, without SSI, it's a lot simpler and faster.)

The Appeals Council Review

What if the ALJ decides you're not disabled?

It happens. They can overturn the state agency decisions—and often do. But that doesn't mean they will believe YOU are disabled.

There is one more level of appeal within the agency. That's the Appeals Council review.

The Appeals Council is in Falls Church Virginia, and they are the only ones with the authority to overturn the ALJ decisions.

The form you need is the SSA-520:

http://www.ssa.gov/online/ha-520.pdf

In many cases, they do so by sending the case back to the local hearings office and telling them to hold a new hearing or make a new decision, which means it will take months for the hearings office to do what they're told.

The Appeals Council takes around two years to make a decision. Maybe now the wait is even longer.

Therefore, SSA generally allows people to file new applications while they are waiting for an Appeals Council decision. However, you cannot use a date of onset earlier than the date of the hearing decision, because that would be disrespecting the ALJ's decision you're not disabled.

For example:

Geri gets an adverse hearing decision dated January 11, 2011. On February 3, 2011 she goes into her local SSA office and files for an Appeals Council review. She also files a new DIB and SSI disability claim with an alleged date of onset of January 12, 2011.

And if you lose your Appeals Council decision? You can sue SSA in court. Talk to your lawyer.

When Should You Get a Lawyer

Contrary to what some SSA lawyers will tell you, you do NOT need a lawyer at the initial claims and reconsideration levels.

These decisions are made by the DDS workers. They are fact-based. They must follow their specific guidelines.

They care what the medical evidence says. They don't give a rip what lawyers say.

For example: if the medical standard for evaluating a particular illness is a test on which you must score 65 or over, and your score is 64, you get denied. Your lawyer can beg and plead all they want that 64 is almost 65, but the state agency worker will follow the guidelines they're given.

And if your test score is 65 or over, you'll be approved without the help of the lawyer.

If you have a lawyer at this point, you'll lose 25% of your back benefits.

I can't think of any good reason to have a lawyer at the initial claims or reconsideration level. They don't do anything for you except delay your decision. They don't complete the forms as well as SSA workers—and they usually just send them in for SSA to complete for them.

If they have one of their clerks try to complete the forms, those clerks do a lousy job and an SSA worker has to recontact you, which delays processing of your appeal.

And some lawyers may have you fill out the forms yourself. You don't need to pay 25% of your back benefits just to be told to do things yourself you can already do for yourself.

And if you can't complete the forms for yourself, you can always go to your local SSA office and have a CR complete them for you, and you pay nothing for that.

In return for getting in the way of the process, often delaying it—sometimes deliberately—if you are approved, lawyers then get 25% of your back pay.

But isn't it worth it to be approved? At the initial claims and reconsideration levels, they don't do anything to help you get approved you can't do yourself. And they'll probably tell you to do it yourself.

Contrary to what some people believe, SSA and the state agencies are not full of blue meanie bureaucrats who deny all claims unless you're smart enough to hire a lawyer in a white hat to ride to your rescue.

SSA and the state agencies are full of people who do the best job possible with the facts available to them. And when they have the facts they use whatever those facts show, no matter what any lawyer says.

That's my opinion on getting a lawyer for an initial claim and reconsideration. If you agree to pay a lawyer 25% of your back pay for claims and reconsideration, you must be trying to get disability for a mental disorder, because you have a screw loose.

When You Do Want a Lawyer

However, if you wind up filing for a hearing, you want a lawyer.

I'm not happy about that, but it's the truth.

The ALJs are lawyers also, so a good Social Security lawyer can talk to the ALJ in a way they both understand.

File the hearing at the SSA office first. You don't need a lawyer to file the paperwork for you to get it started. If you let them handle it, they may delay it—even past the 60 day appeal period.

Once your hearing is on record with SSA, however, getting a good lawyer is your second step.

When you file for a hearing, the SSA field office is supposed to give you a list of local Social Security specialist lawyers, including your local Legal Services.

How do you tell you who is good and who sucks?

That's tough. SSA workers have definite opinions, but are not allowed to express them.

The ideal would be to find out which lawyers the ALJs like the most, but you'll never know that. Even I as a CR had no clue as to what the ALJs thought.

One guideline I can give you is, don't go with a law firm that advertises for personal injury claims but also does Social Security work on the side. If a law firm runs ads that remind you of Denzel Washington in the movie PHILADELPHIA, move on.

You do want a lawyer that does only SSA work, because they'll be more likely to have vocational experts and other medical experts they can call as witnesses if necessary. They're more likely to have relationships with all the local ALJs. They're more likely to know about and understand the technicalities of Title 2 date of onset, and also about SSI.

And you do want a lawyer or a professional disability representative—an industry started by Allsup. Do not go with some friend or neighbor who bought a "disability representative" home business kit out of the back pages of a biz op magazine or off a web page.

And of course do NOT go with anybody who sends you unsolicited email.

I suggest trying to find your local members of the National Organization of Social Security Claimants' Representatives. Their web site is:

http://www.nosscr.org/

But you need to actually call them to find members in your area. Their phone number is 1-800-431-2804.

You can probably gather from things I say in this book I do not have an overall positive view of Social Security lawyers, and that assumption is accurate. I will say of the lawyers I dealt with who seemed to be the best were associated with that organization.

Joining the NOSSCR is not a guarantee a lawyer will be good, but it's the best you can do short of getting the uncensored viewpoints of the ALJs in your local hearings office, and that won't happen.

Prototype States

In 1999 SSA decided to perform an experiment. They did away with the reconsideration step of the appeals process in "prototype" states. It was believed, because state agency workers often reach the same conclusion about a case, it would allow people to get a faster approval by going straight to the hearing level.

What happened is some people—especially people who missed their CE but who are now willing to attend a CE—who could have been quickly approved by a reconsideration handled by the state disability office now had to wait a year or two for a hearings decision.

People who would have been denied at the reconsideration level do save a few months by going to the hearing first.

Because of the increase in the hearings workload, however, the hearings offices got farther behind than they were before.

The prototype states are: Alabama, Alaska, Colorado, Louisiana, Michigan, Missouri, New Hampshire, and Pennsylvania.

(If your claim is not in one of these ten states, this does not apply to you.)

If your disability claim is denied in one of those states, you do not have the right to request a reconsideration. Your first level of appeal is the hearing.

I've read that the new 2011 government budget is restoring the reconsideration level of appeal to those states, beginning with Michigan in 2011.

One Sign You Really Ought to File an Appeal:

The state agency tells you that you can perform jobs in the national economy you've never heard of.

I've seen them tell people they can be a "dipper."

What's a dipper? I don't know. In three decades of asking people about their work histories, I don't recall anybody who told me they ever actually worked as a dipper.

It would make sense to tell people they can still take orders at McDonald's or mop floors for office buildings, but instead they tell people to be dippers.

Continuing Disability Reviews (CDRs)

Well, Social Security decided you are disabled and finally got your monthly disability checks started. You're now set for life, right?

Errr, not quite.

That does seem to be the general attitude. People believe once they're found disabled, they should be able to collect checks until they die. And in many cases that does happen.

But it's not guaranteed.

Remember the disability journal and work journal I advised you to write before you applied, and keep up to date after filing your application?

Keep them up to date.

While receiving monthly disability benefit checks can seem like the end of a long process to you, it may actually be just the beginning of a very long relationship between you and your local Social Security office.

SSA has the legal right—and obligation—to make sure people on disability benefits continue to be disabled, or to have their checks discontinued.

By law, when the state agency makes a determination you're disabled, they also set a medical review diary.

Most of these are for three years. That means that three years from then, SSA should be contacting you to do a continuing disability review (CDR). That is a review to see whether or not your disability continues.

For some people in extremely bad condition, the diary is set for 7 years.

For some people who can be expected to get medically better quickly, the diary is set for 1 year.

A few people are so severely disabled they'll never have a CDR. But if you can hear at all, see at all, walk at all and read these words, you probably don't fall into that category.

Some people are simply sent a form SSA-455 to complete themselves in the mail. Based on what you say on that form, you may be or may not be scheduled for a complete CDR.

These medical CDRs are much like filing for disability all over again, only your monthly benefits continue through the process. (SSA will not stop your benefits while it processes your CDR.)

The interview may be conducted in person or over the telephone. The field office will complete with you form SSA-454 Continuing Disability Review Report:

http://www.disabilityfacts.com/resources/Forms/FORM_SSA_454-BK.pdf

As I mentioned, it's essentially like applying all over again, only you do continue to receive checks every month. You'll be asked about your medical condition, whether it's gotten better or worse since your benefits began, whether you have any new medical problems, everywhere you've been treated in the past year, and what medicines you're taking now.

You'll also be asked if you've worked since you got on disability benefits. If so, they'll complete an SSA-821 asking you a lot of questions about it. Or they'll complete an SSA-820 if you've been self-employed.

They'll also ask about whether you have received any additional education or vocational training since you got on disability.

If your medical records are not complete enough to make a medical decision, they will send you to a consultative exam. Make sure you attend it, or they'll assume you must not be disabled any longer.

The CDR will be sent to the state agency to make the medical decision. That worker must determine whether or not your condition has improved enough since your last medical decision you could perform SGA.

If not, they'll decide you are still disabled. You'll get a notice to that effect, and that's the end of it for at least three more years.

If the state agency decides your medical condition has improved to the point where you can perform SGA, you are no longer disabled. Therefore, they will send you a notice your disability check is going to stop in a couple of months. (They are not supposed to make you overpaid.)

You have the usual 60 days to file for an appeal. However, if you believe you are still disabled, it would be stupid to wait that long.

If you file an appeal within the first 15 days of the date of the notice, you have the right to request your checks continue while the appeal is processed. If you believe you are disabled and you need the money, why would you wait more than one business day?

I don't know, but many people do.

Age 18 CDRs

One special type of CDR is the SSI Age 18 review.

In 1992 the Supreme Court of the United States settled a class action lawsuit (Zebley vs Sullivan) against SSA by ordering it to declare children filing for SSI disabled using easier standards than those applied to adults.

SSA has to follow the Supreme Court's rulings. However, they reacted wisely (for once), in my opinion.

They implemented a policy of having all SSI children undergo a CDR right around their 18th birthdays, when they become adults and therefore are no longer affected by the Supreme Court ruling.

If you are receiving SSI for a child, about the time of their 18th birthday, you should get a letter asking you to bring them in person into your local office.

The CR you speak with will have to ask a lot of questions. Among them will be the CDR.

The CR will complete an SSA-3368 the same as though they were an adult just applying for disability. If the child has ever worked, the CR will also complete an SSA-821.

The information is then sent to the state agency, who evaluates the child based on the criteria of an adult.

I saw some 18 year olds who obviously were still severely retarded. Some were retarded when they were kids, but seemed to have grown into reasonably intelligent adults who didn't even know why they were called "disabled" and wanted to work like their friends. Some didn't seem to think of themselves as disabled, but thought they were entitled to a government check for the rest of their lives anyway, just because they wanted it. Some were impressive testaments to the special education programs they attended.

Sometimes the biggest problem was discussing all this with the mothers who'd been using the kid's check to pay all the bills and were now financially threatened by the possibility it could stop in a few months.

Work CDRs

This applies to Social Security, not SSI.

If you are receiving DIB benefits and you return to work, each month you work and make at least $720 (as of 2012), that month is called one of your "trial work months."

Once you have 9 trial work months (whether you do it in 9 months straight or work one month a year for 9 years), SSA has to do a work CDR on you. That mean evaluating your work to determine whether or not you have proven you can do SGA for a sustained period (by actually doing it.)

These evaluations are complicated. You can't do it yourself. What you should do is report any and all work you do right away to SSA, and keep all your paystubs so you have an accurate record of how much money you received in each calendar month.

However, don't be scared to work.

SSA has rules that allow people whose checks are stopped for doing SGA to have the checks resumed if their work falls below SGA.

It's called the Extended Period of Eligibility, and it's complicated.

For one thing, your Medicare coverage continues for 93 months (7 years and 9 months). Many disabled people fear having Medicare coverage stopped more than their checks stopped, because they don't qualify for regular medical insurance. They may well prefer working to sitting at home, but need their medical treatment.

If your work goes below SGA within 3 years, your benefits are reinstated without filing a brand new application. So you don't have to wait for a new medical decision.

This applies to Social Security DIB only. SSI recipients cannot have their benefits cut off for doing SGA (though wages do reduce SSI checks—and can cut them off if the wages are high enough—as explained in the income chapter.)

Can or Should You Request a CDR?

What if you've been on disability for three years or longer but SSA has never contacted you for a CDR, either by mail or over the phone or by asking you to come into the office?

Don't do anything until you're asked to.

Maybe it's because you have a very severe, permanent disability and you'll never need a CDR.

Maybe it's because they are behind. The agency is chronically short of staff, and some offices are in worse shape than others. Some have a large backlog. You may be in that backlog. It's not your problem.

What you should do is make sure SSA has your correct mailing address.

One day you get the CDR mailer form 455. Or one day it may be a letter asking you to call or come into the office for some other reason. Or telling you have an appointment at a particular time to be called or to come in.

Keep such appointments if at all possible. If not, notify SSA right away. Don't wait until the appointment time is in the past.

If you don't respond to a first such notice, SSA normally sends a certified letter to follow up.

If you get a green receipt in the mail notifying you of certified mail, go to the Post Office and claim it right away. It's amazing how often people refuse to do this, and then whine about how they didn't get the notice. They didn't get the notice because they failed to go to the Post Office to get it.

Sometimes the certified letter is received at the house. The Post Office sends it back to SSA with a signature. Who knows who signed? A young teenager? A neighbor? A home health aide?

If you allow anybody to go to the front door to get your mail for you, you better make sure they give you any certified mail they sign for. If the Post Office returns the green receipt to SSA with a signature, SSA will assume you got the certified letter. If you don't respond to it, you're deliberately ignoring SSA, and that does get your check stopped for failure to cooperate.

The above paragraphs are a repeat, because they're important enough to repeat.

A Voluntary Report of Medical Improvement

SSA will also do CDRs on people who come in to report their medical condition has improved.

How many times did I hear somebody report that? If you had to use any fingers, you counted too high. Zero.

Medicare 101

Medicare was created in 1965 by President Lyndon Baines Johnson.

It's an insurance program, which means it has some complexities, but can be understood piece by piece.

First of all, you start getting Medicare 4 ways:

1. You turn age 65, you are insured, you're getting some kind of RSI benefit (RIB, spouse's or DWB), or Railroad benefit, or could be, or you are not insured but you elect to pay the premium

(Coverage starts with the first day of the month you turn 65.)

2. You receive Title 2 DIB benefits for 2 years (because of the 5 month waiting period, this effectively means you go on DIB 2 1/2 years after your date of onset).

3. You have end stage renal disease, which means you're on dialysis or have received a kidney transplant

4. You have ALS (Amyotrophic Lateral Sclerosis, also called Lou Gehrig's disease), which means you get Medicare Parts A and B the month your disability benefits begin.

If you meet #3, you should work with a social worker at your hospital or clinic. They probably have a set procedure for having SSA take your application. If not, go to your local SSA office immediately.

If you meet #2, you are put on Medicare automatically when you reach that time.

If you meet #1 and are drawing benefits, you'll go on Medicare automatically.

If you meet #1 and you are not yet drawing benefits (say you're still working and not yet retired), you can file for Medicare.

Also, many government employees are eligible for Medicare as of age 65 even though they are not insured, because they began paying into the Medicare trust fund out of their paychecks early in the 1980s.

There are many ins and outs. If you are 65 and not receiving RSI benefits and not insured, you should still go into your local office (I wouldn't try this by Internet even if it's technically available) and put in an application. You may be eligible for deemed insured Medicare. At the worst, you'll have to make monthly payments ($451 per month as of 2012). Bring in your birth certificate to prove your age.

Apply three months before you turn age 65.

If you wait until the three months after you turn 65, you'll lose Part B benefits.

If you don't sign up in the seven month initial enrollment period (the three months before you turn 65, the month you turn 65 and the three months after you turn 65), you have to wait until the General Enrollment period, which is from January 1 through March 31 of every year. Your coverage will begin July 1 of that year.

If you don't sign up when first eligible and you have to pay the premium, your premium will be even higher.

If you don't sign up for Part B when first eligible, you may have to pay higher premiums for it the rest of your life once you do sign up.

There are 3 basic sections of Medicare:

Part A (HI) - Hospitalization—for "covered inpatient hospital, post-hospital extended care, and home health services."

Unless you are not insured and must pay a monthly payment, there is no out of your pocket cost to receive Part A HI benefits. There are deductibles, and they don't pay 100% of all expenses, though.

Part B (SMI)—Supplementary Medical Insurance—pays or helps pay for services from doctors not covered under Part A.

This section is voluntary, because there is a charge. Wherever possible, SSA takes your SMI premiums out of your Social Security, Railroad or Civil Service benefit checks. If you don't receive such a monthly check, you can make monthly payments.

As of 2012 the monthly premium for most SMI enrollees is $99.90 a month. It can go up every year depending on the cost of running the Medicare premium (which is not likely to get cheaper any time soon).

Part D—Prescription Drug coverage—This began just a few years ago. It covers a lot of the cost of prescription drugs. It is a new and separate part of the program, requiring a new and separate monthly premium.

I put Medicare Part C—Medicare Advantage—out of order because it's not really part of Medicare. It is Medicare coverage through approved private insurance companies which offer Medicare Advantage plans. They cover everything, so you don't need—and cannot be sold—a Medigap policy.

For more information contact:

1-800-633-4227

TTY 1-877-486-2048

http://www.medicare.gov

This pamphlet may help you also:

http://www.medicare.gov/publications/pubs/pdf/10050.pdf

Medicare Part A - HI Hospitalization Insurance

This portion of Medicare covers the basic medical costs of being hospitalized. That includes a skilled nursing facility (though not custodial or long-term care), hospice and home health care.

There are a lot of various rules. Medicare will pay for a semi-private room but not a private room unless medically necessary. If there's a separate charge for telephone and television service, they are not covered.

You must be an inpatient, which means admitted by a doctor. If you're there overnight just because it took that long to be seen in the emergency room, you're still an outpatient and that's not covered by Part A.

Part A also covers general hospital nursing care, hospital supplies and medicine included as part of your stay. It doesn't cover private duty nursing.

It also does not include services from a doctor while you're there. (Though those can be covered by Part B if you have that as well.)

Hospice care usually does not mean Medicare will pay for you to stay full-time in a hospice facility. It usually means you get hospice care at your home or nursing home where you live.

You cannot assume Medicare will cover 100% of these charges. Copayments, deductibles and coinsurance do apply.

If you need skilled nursing care after staying in a hospital at least three days, Medicare will cover that. But it will not pay for ordinary long term care in a nursing home.

Basically, with Medicare Part A you have the confidence if you get sick or injured, you can receive inpatient services at a hospital.

Supplemental Medical Insurance (SMI) - Part B

This is the part of Medicare health insurance which pays for services from a doctor, especially outpatient services for going to see a doctor, or for being in the emergency room.

It can cover seeing the doctor, tests, medical equipment, home health services (you have to be in such bad shape you can't leave home without help - you have to be unable to drive yourself to the doctor's office, for example).

Part B also covers some preventative services. This is a new trend, and a good one.

Copayments, coinsurance and deductibles can and do apply. So do various rules connected with some of the services and tests.

For example, you must pay all the deductible in a year before Medicare will start paying for any tests or services. As of 2012, the Part B annual deductible is $140.

The list of services takes up many pages. If you want a particular service, look it up on the chart and discuss it with your doctor. They have to order everything anyway.

https://questions.medicare.gov/app/answers/detail/a_id/48/~/what-types-of-services-are-covered-under-medicare%3F

My only comment is if you are a smoker, you really ought to take advantage of the smoking cessation counseling services now available.

You may want services Medicare doesn't cover. You will have to pay for them yourself or be under a private insurance plan that covers them:

This includes:

Long term care

Routine dental care, including dentures

Cosmetic surgery

Acupuncture

Hearing aids and hearing aid exams

Chiropractic services except spinal manipulation to correct a subluxation. (I don't know what that means, but if you have a chiropractor do anything else, Medicare will not pay for it.)

IRMA is a Socialist B*TCH

Several years ago, Congress passed a law requiring people who receive more money, to pay more money for Medicare Part B premiums. This does contradict the social insurance (instead of welfare) principles Social Security was founded on, and I believe it's a harbinger of the future to try to keep the system going by taxing the rich.

Here's how it works:

Every year the Social Security Administration has to calculate the actual cost of Part B SMI per recipient. Most people then pay 25% of the total cost out of their Social Security checks and the Medicare trust fund makes up the difference. As mentioned before, in 2012 this monthly premium was $99.90.

That basically means that if Part B came from a private insurance company, its premium would be 4 X 99.90 = $399.60 per month.

By paying only 25%, most people get a bargain.

But the government is (correctly so in my opinion) worried about the financial health of the trust funds, and therefore a few years ago decided to make people with higher than average incomes pay more than 25%.

They look at the total income on your tax return two years ago. If it was higher than average (now defined as $85,000 for one person), then your Part B SMI premium will be higher than average.

Here's the chart for 2011:

Your income in 2009:	Your 2011 SMI Premium:
$85,001 to $107,000	$161.50
$107,001 to $160,000	$230.70
$160,001 to $214,000	$299.90
$214,000+	$369.10

If you're married and filing a joint return, the income amounts are doubled. The SMI premiums come out of each of your SSA checks.

Sometimes people's circumstances and income change. If you're now paying a high SMI premium because of a one-time event in 2009 that boosted your income far above average, report it to Social Security. Also report changes in your marital status such as divorce, separation or death of a spouse.

Medicaid Pays the Part B SMI Premium

If you're on the other end of income spectrum and therefore qualify for Medicaid, that will pay for your Part B SMI premium.

As soon as your enrollment in Part B begins, notify your caseworker so they can start the paperwork for Medicaid to pay your SMI premium to Social Security instead of it coming out of your check.

This makes financial sense for the Medicaid agency. They pay $99.90 a month, and then Medicare—not them—pays most of your health care costs.

If you are on Medicaid, it basically acts as your "Medigap" insurance because it covers most everything that Medicare doesn't. (But check with your local Medicaid agency for details.)

Medicare Part D - Prescription Drugs

This is the most recent addition to the Medicare program, passed by President George W Bush in 2006. It's the first new federal entitlement program created in many years.

As such, it's still controversial. I've heard justifications that make some sense. When Medicare was originally created in 1965, medical science did not have the extensive number of prescription drugs to effectively control chronic medical conditions they have now.

Medicare Part A would pay tens of thousands of dollars for a diabetic to have a foot amputated...but not pay for the insulin or other medication that may have controlled the diabetes so the foot never had to be amputated. So it makes more economic sense to pay for monthly medicine so people could avoid expensive surgery in the future.

Whether it's working out that way or not, I can't say.

However, many seniors and disabled people now save a lot of money on their prescription medications.

You can start on Part D when you start Parts A and B when you're either 65, on DIB for two years or suffer from end stage renal disease or ALS. That is, during your initial enrollment period.

If you are covered by other insurance with prescription drug coverage that's at least as good as Part D, you can delay signing up for Part D. However, if you delay signing up for Part D and you don't have the same or better coverage with another insurance provider, you'll pay a penalty when you do sign up for Part D.

If you don't want to pay the premium because you're not on many prescription drugs, I applaud you. I'm not 65 yet, but last year when I had my first checkups in years, the medical staff were all amazed I wasn't taking any ongoing prescription medicines.

Though, to me, that's a sad commentary on the health of others my age.

However, if you don't sign up when you're first eligible, you're taking a risk. I don't take ongoing drugs, but I've needed antibiotics several times in the past year, and for pneumonia three years ago. I'm generally healthy, but not bullet-proof, and neither are you.

Part D is basically a separate form of medical insurance requiring a separate premium. The premiums are taken out of your Social Security, Railroad or Civil Service checks just like Part B SMI premiums.

The amounts can vary, however.

This is one of the confusing parts of Part D. In every state, insurance companies offer you various plans, and you have to choose the plan best for you.

They can vary according to what they charge as a monthly premium, what they charge as a copayment for particular medications, and what pharmacies they are available at.

The monthly premium for Company A may be $25 and for Company B $40. However, maybe Company A charges $18 for a bottle of Furosemide and Company B charges only $7 for the same bottle of Furosemide.

There is no easy way to calculate this, except to go online with a list of your medications, and analyze exactly how much each company will cost you and go with the cheapest—assuming they are available at your preferred pharmacy. If you don't have a preferred pharmacy, you'll still want to make sure your Part D provider is available close to your home.

Besides, the plans could change next year.

And your medications could change in the future.

If you decide to change to a different plan, you can do so during open season of November 15 through December 31 of every year.

And the class warfare warriors have also gotten to Part D. If you receive more income (as determined by your tax return two years ago) than they think you should, they want you to pay more than most people.

The income ranges are the same as for Part B SMI premiums.

Here's the chart:

Your 2009 Taxable Income:	Your 2011 Monthly Part D Premium:
$85,000 or less	Your Plan Premium
$85,001 to $107,000	$12.00 + Your Plan Premium
$107,001 to $160,000	$31.10 + Your Plan Premium
$160,001 up to $214,	$50.10 + Your Plan Premium
$214,001+	$69.10 + Your Plan Premium

Again, those amounts are doubled for married couples filing joint returns.

Many plans, though not all, have a deductible you must meet before they start paying for your drugs for the year. You can assume, just as with all other kinds of insurance, the lower the deductible, the higher the monthly premium.

You will also have to make a copayment to the pharmacy. This will be a lot less than the full price of the medicine, however.

You may have heard people talk of the "donut hole." This is a coverage "gap" where the Part D plan provider will not pay for your medicines.

A typical plan will have a deductible, which you must pay first.

Then there will be a large amount where they will pay most of the costs of the drugs.

Then there will be the coverage gap where they won't pay for anything.

Then once you've paid a certain amount, they will begin paying again.

Not everybody reaches that coverage gap. In most plans it's quite high. But if you take large amounts of expensive prescription drugs, you might reach it. In that case, you must be prepared to pay a few thousand dollars out of your own pocket.

But to protect people with really expensive drug needs, at some point Part D kicks back in. That's known as catastrophic coverage. If you run through the coverage gap within a year, you're taking a very large amount of expensive prescription medications.

This donut hole coverage was criticized as soon as the law was originally passed. The law has been modified to reduce the coverage gap, and eliminate it by 2020.

If you reach the coverage gap in 2011 you get a 50% discount on name brand prescription drugs. Medicare suggests you talk to your doctor to make sure you're taking the least expensive drugs for your condition.

Extra Help for People With Low Income and Resources

If you want Medicare Part D but feel you cannot afford to pay the premium, you can apply for a benefit called Extra Help. This is basically a needs based program included as part of the Part D package.

Extra Help will pay some or all of your Medicare Part D monthly premium if you meet certain requirements.

If you receive SSI or Medicaid, you automatically qualify for Extra Help.

As of 2011, if you are single you may qualify if your income is below $16,335 and your resources are below $12,640.

If you are married you may qualify if your combined incomes are below $22,065 and your combined resources are below $25,260.

Resource rules are similar to SSI. A house where you reside, a car, household goods and life insurance policies are all excluded.

However, if you have certificates of deposit paying you thousands of dollars in interest per year, please don't bother applying for this. You are over the limit and your application will be denied. It just wastes your time and SSA's, and makes you look like a scammer which, at your age, I hope you don't want.

Yes, some people who obviously own a lot of money tried to rip off the system.

State Health Insurance Assistance Programs (SHIP)

The federal government gives State Health Insurance Assistance Programs money to give free health insurance counseling to people with Medicare. They are not connected with Medicare, Social Security, the government or any insurance company or health plan. They are staffed by volunteers, so get the information you need but be nice to them.

They will help inform you about your Medicare rights, complaints about medical care or treatment, billing problems and plan choices.

They can help you decide which Part D Plan Provider would best meet your needs.

They can help you decide whether you should go with Original Medicare or sign up for a Medicare Advantage Plan.

Here is the link to the telephone numbers of the state SHIP offices:

http://www.medicare.gov/contacts/organization-search-criteria.aspx

You must select "SHIP - State Health Insurance Assistance Program" on the first drop down menu, and your particular state in the second.

Medicare Advantage

This is an attempt to provide further benefits for the elderly and disabled by allowing private insurance companies to manage the Medicare programs. It goes back to 1997 under another name, and the concept was revised and renamed by a law in 2003.

They are approved by Medicare. They can offer additional services such as:

* Free preventative care
* Filling the Part D pharmaceutical benefit "donut hole"
* Dental and vision plans
* Health club memberships

Paying for the gap in Medicare Part D prescription drug coverage is a benefit many seniors, especially those with very high medicine expenses, want.

And if you are under one of these plans, you don't need a Medigap policy.

And so far these plans have been subsidized by up to 18% by the Medicare trust fund.

Therefore, in effect, people on these plans are being indirectly subsidized.

Therefore, I've seen estimates from one-fifth to one-fourth of seniors are now under a Medicare Advantage Plan rather than original Medicare.

If you're approached by one of their salespeople, you must get all the information you can to determine whether Medicare Advantage and any particular plan is right for you.

You Have the Choice of Getting "Original" Medicare or Signing Up for an All in One Medicare Advantage Plan Where You Get Everything as a Package Deal

The choice is yours.

If you currently go to a doctor or hospital or clinic where you are happy, check with them to see if they are under any particular plan.

With a Medicare Advantage Plan, you will probably be restricted to their medical providers.

With Original Medicare, you can use any medical provider that accepts it.

I don't have any statistics. Sometimes doctors get mad at Medicare because of the rules and bureaucratic paperwork involved, and don't want to accept it. However, the vast majority of older patients have Medicare and wish to use it, even if they can afford to pay more than ordinary patients.

Unless a doctor specializes in services Medicare doesn't cover (cosmetic surgeons) or has patients not covered by Medicare (pediatricians), I don't see how they can get by not accepting it.

But check with your personal doctor to be sure.

Some Medicare Advantage plans provide services original Medicare doesn't, but they may charge extra for them.

All I can say is, be very careful. Ask a lot of questions. Make sure you're getting everything you want for a price you can afford, and there are no problems buried in the fine print.

If everything looks good to you, go ahead. You can change later on, during late year open season. That's October 15 through December 7.

If you have a doctor, clinic or hospital where you want to continue going, check out any plan with them.

And see if they accept assignment. That means they accept whatever Medicare pays for a particular service. Sometimes they want more money, and will charge you for what Medicare doesn't pay.

Obviously, if two doctors are equally good, but one accepts assignment and the other one doesn't, you're best off with the one that accepts assignment.

If you do not get a Medicare Advantage Plan, you may be interested in Medigap insurance. This is a supplemental insurance that pays everything, such as deductibles, Medicare does not.

It is expensive, but if you ever have a severe medical condition it can be worth it.

The last six months of her life, my mother received a large amount of medical services. But all she ever had to pay was a nominal deductible for prescription drugs from her pharmacy.

If she and the rest of her family had had to worry about how to pay for everything, that time would have been even more stressful than it was.

The best time to sign up for Medigap insurance is within the six months following the month you turn 65, so plan ahead.

This booklet has more advice from Medicare regarding Medigap policies:

http://go.usa.gov/lot

Supplemental Security Income (SSI)

In 1972 President Richard M. Nixon signed the law authorizing Title XVI of the Social Security Act. It went into effect January 1, 1974.

The intent of the law was so make blind, disabled and old age assistance welfare benefits more equitable across the United States. Their rules and payment amounts varied from state to state.

The Social Security Administration was chosen to administer this new federal program. This made sense because it would require many public offices across the United States—which SSA already had in place. Plus SSA was already making disability determinations of its own for DIB applicants. And it was already making date of birth determinations for its RIB applicants.

Therefore, it was relatively easy to add SSI to its workload.

The basic function of SSI is to provide people with just enough money to provide their food and shelter—if they're not getting it from other sources.

As much as possible, SSA pays SSI benefits so everyone receiving SSI is getting basically the same amount of money.

You'll see how that works in the income chapter.

Three Categories of SSI

To get SSI you must fall into one of three categories:

1. Age 65 or older

2. Disabled (same as DIB, except excludes blindness)

3. Blind

Notice in this program, unlike Title 2, disability and blindness are two separate categories. Being blind for SSI purposes says nothing about your ability to work.

Notice I wrote YOU must fall into one of those three categories. SSI is a needs based program. It pays only those people who meet the requirements. It does not pay any dependents. Sometimes mothers come in and want to file for SSI for children because their father is on SSI. If their father is on SSI, he is not supporting the child anyway, so the child is not really his dependent.

However, unlike DIB, there is no minimum age to be found disabled or blind for SSI. The program pays many children who have been found disabled (or blind).

Children are evaluated according to their own criteria. That rarely includes work, obviously, except for a few 16 and 17 year old applicants who have worked prior to applying.

Because of the Zebley vs Sullivan Supreme Court case 1992, it's actually easier for children to be found disabled than adults.

Then you must meet the other requirements:

1. US Citizen, Alien admitted as refugee within 7 years of entering the US, and other aliens under a system so complicated it's beyond belief

Once upon a time, all US citizens and lawfully admitted for permanent residence aliens were eligible. Aliens lawfully admitted into the US prior to August 22, 1996 still have "grandfather" rights.

The Welfare Reform Act wiped out most alien eligibility and replaced it with a system incredibly confusing and complicated. You may qualify if you've worked forty quarters under FICA, served in the US Armed Forces, or been a victim of abuse. Or you're a child and one of your parents meets those criteria.

Aliens admitted into the US as refugees could receive SSI for up to five years, then were cut off on the theory after 5 years they were eligible to become citizens. However, the INS and its successors in Department of Homeland Security are so far behind in processing naturalization requests Congress had to give the refugees two more years.

Basically, if you're an alien in the US your best move for SSI is to become a citizen as soon as possible.

2. Residing in the United States

You can leave the US temporarily, but if you remain outside the US for more than 30 days, you're not eligible for SSI until you have returned for over 30 days.

3. Not residing in a public institution

If you're in a public institution such as a state hospital, a jail etc, you are already living off the taxpayers and so are not due additional taxpayer money.

(NOTE TO THOSE STILL IN JAIL: If you have one of those letters telling you that you're automatically eligible for SSI upon release from jail, you can throw it away because it's not worth the paper it's printed on. I first saw one when I was a trainee, and prisoners were still bringing them in before I left the agency. It's worthless. Once out of jail, you can apply for SSI disability the same as anybody else, but you must also meet the medical tests, and the need requirements, the same as everybody else. You do not qualify for SSI just because you got out of jail.)

This does not include students at state-owned universities.

4. Under the resource limit

In 1974 the SSI resource limit was $1,500 for individuals and $2,250 for couples. Years later it was changed to $2,000 for individuals and $3,000 for couples.

It could change, but probably will not change again soon. Obviously, that means in effect inflation has slightly reduced it.

Resources is a huge topic deserving of its own chapter.

5. Under the income limit

This changes most every year with a Cost of Living Allowance (COLA) based on the rate of inflation.

In 1974 it was $140 per month for individuals, $210 a month for couples.

As of 2012 it is $698 per month for individuals and $1048 for couples.

Income is also a huge topic that needs its own chapter.

State Supplementation

Although the SSI law was designed to eliminate inequity in old age, disability and blindness payments across the country, it actually preserved that to some extent, because it gives states the right to pay SSI beneficiaries extra money on top of what the federal government pays.

Right now, these states pay extra to the SSI beneficiaries residing in them:

* California
* The District Of Columbia
* Hawaii
* Massachusetts
* Nevada

* New Jersey
* New York
* Pennsylvania
* Rhode Island
* Vermont

You MUST reside within those states to receive their supplemental payments.

By far the most generous state is California, and always has been. I worked in states that did not have any state supplement payments. Sometimes I'd interview someone who just arrived from California and were reporting their change of address. Many of them, once they learned what their check would go down to—immediately returned to California.

Presumptive Disability (SSI Only)

Because SSI is based on need, SSA and the state agencies make a special effort to get checks started as early as possible when this is feasible.

If SSA can verify the applicant has a medical condition so severe approval is almost guaranteed, SSA will start paying checks for up to six months. The final paperwork still takes time, but SSA can get checks started.

This is one benefit of SSI over DIB, where there is no presumption of need.

If a person's disability falls into one of the below categories, and it can be verified, then the CR should take a full claims application from you and request all necessary proofs.

Verification varies depending on the condition. They can use visual confirmation for someone being in a wheelchair, for example. But AIDS requires special forms completed by a doctor to record how severe it is.

The official list is:

Amputation of a leg at the hip

Allegation of total deafness; that is, no sound perception in either ear

Allegation of total blindness; that is, no light perception in either eye

Allegation of bed confinement and immobility due to a longstanding condition

Allegation of stroke (cerebral vascular accident) more than 3 months in the past and continued marked difficulty in walking or using a hand or arm

Allegation of cerebral palsy, muscular dystrophy or muscle atrophy, and marked difficulty in walking (e.g., the use of braces), speaking, or coordination of the hands or arms

Allegation of Down syndrome

Allegation of severe mental deficiency for child at least 7 years of age

A child under one year old had a birth weight below 1200 grams (2 pounds, 10 ounces) at birth.

Symptomatic human immunodeficiency virus (HIV) infection or acquired immunodeficiency syndrome (AIDS) Form SSA-4814 or SSA-4815 is needed.

A child under one year old and fell within one of following combinations of gestational age (GA) at birth with birth-weight:

GA: 37-40 weeks—Weight at Birth: Less than 2000 grams (4 pounds, 6 ounces)

GA: 36 weeks—Weight at Birth: 1875 grams or less (4 pounds, 2 ounces)

GA: 35 weeks—Weight at Birth: 1700 grams or less (3 pounds, 12 ounces)

GA: 34 weeks—Weight at Birth: 1500 grams or less (3 pounds, 5 ounces)

GA: 33 weeks—Weight at Birth: At least 1200 grams, but no more than 1325 grams (2 pounds, 15 ounces)

Terminally ill - life expectancy below six months

Spinal cord injury producing an inability to ambulate without the use of a walker or bilateral hand-held assistive devices

End stage renal disease (ESRD) requiring chronic dialysis

Amyotrophic lateral sclerosis (ALS)—Lou Gehrig's disease

In my experience most of these are quite rare. By far, the most common is low birth weight babies.

If you fall into one of the above categories, you want to give SSA the proof as quickly as possible.

However, you also need to provide proofs of nondisability issues immediately.

You want to be paid quickly. The CR wants to pay you quickly (because it improves their processing time and makes them look better to their boss).

So if they ask you for wages check stubs, life insurance policies, bank statements or anything else, bring them in right away.

People complain a lot about how long it takes for SSA to process disability cases, and most of those complaints are justified.

However, in the case of presumptive disability (and presumptive blindness), the agency is trying to pay you as quickly as possible.

If you don't provide requested documentation, the delay is on you.

More Often, the State Agency Makes the Presumptive Disability Decision

The above categories are for people filing initial claims.

If you don't have one of the above conditions (most of which are rare), you don't immediately qualify for PD payments.

However, many times the state agency will see from some medical records the person is going to be an allowance once all paperwork and processing is completed, which will take additional time. They will then notify the CR, who will then contact you to develop a full SSI application.

This is up to the judgment of the state agency worker.

PD is Not a Guarantee of a Final Allowance

In most cases, people who get PD payments are approved at the final determination.

However, this is not a guarantee. If you're receiving PD checks, don't think you have it "in the bag." You don't. Continue to cooperate with all requests for forms and evidence. If they send you to a consultative exam, make you sure you go.

It's unusual for PD cases to have a final denial decision, but it does happen, especially if you don't provide what you're required to.

PD Checks are Not Overpayments

If the final decision on your case is a denial, what about the PD checks you receive?

Ordinarily, when people get money they're not eligible for, it's an overpayment and SSA tries to collect it.

However, PD checks are not considered an overpayment.

Resources

For SSI purposes, a resource is any form of money or property which can be converted to cash to spend on food and shelter.

If it's not convertible to cash, it's not a resource.

The current resource limit is $2,000 for individuals and $3,000 for couples.

Examples of countable resources include:

Cash

Money in a checking or savings account

Stocks, bonds and other securities held in an ordinary brokerage account

An IRA (So what if you're not retired yet? You're starving so withdraw the money. Besides, if you're disabled there is no penalty for withdrawal before age 59 1/2)

Land where you do not live

Jewelry (besides a wedding ring)

Cash surrender value of life insurance policies

Second+ cars

Antiques

Certificates of Deposit (yes, if you cash it in early you'll pay a penalty of interest. If you're really starving—pay the penalty!)

Examples of resources SSA does not count include:

Wedding rings

House and all adjoining land (including large farms) where you reside

First automobile up to a value of $4,500

Ordinary personal and household items up to $3,500

(This figure means what you would get if you sold stuff now—secondhand—not what you originally paid for it. Most CRs will accept your No answer to this question unless you give them reason to believe you have something unusually valuable. If you want to brag how your computer, costume jewelry or a bedroom suite are worth over $3,500 even though they're used, be prepared to take them to a dealer to verify their value.)

A 401(k) plan where you or a spouse are still working (while the worker is still employed, money cannot be withdrawn from these plans, although you can get loans on them)

Something that's worthless—100 shares of stock of a bankrupt business

Ownership interest in a family plot of land which cannot—according to the state law—be sold independently

(This is a big one. There are gazillions of pieces of land in this country—houses and country land—still in the name of Great-great-grandpa and Great-great-grandma, according to the tax records. So long as someone pays the taxes, the tax assessment bureaus don't care.

But the original owners are long dead. Of course they left no will, because they didn't trust lawyers. Their children didn't want to pay a lawyer. Now their children have grandchildren scattered all over the country. In many cases, they all have a legal ownership interest in the property.

In some states, they have the right to sell their ownership interest independently of the rest of the family. In other states they don't.

In states where they do have the right to sell their separate ownership interest, SSA will often request information about the entire structure of heirs—and the SSI applicant may not even know who half their cousins are, let alone where they live. In many cases they've never even seen the property. But SSA needs to verify the fair market value of the property.

And of course, anybody who would buy a one-forty-seventh ownership interest in an old family cabin in the woods must be nuts as well.

If state law says the family members can't sell their interest separately, the land can't be sold without the entire family signing for the sale. Good luck. And then the property is not countable to SSI recipients because they can't convert their ownership interest into cash.

My advice: if you have ownership interest in some family land where you do not live and do not wish to live, yet in that state you have the right to sell it, try to sell it. Try to sell it to another family member. If that doesn't work, try to engage a local real estate agent to sell it for you on the open market.

Keep all paperwork and documentation. That's your proof your 1/47th ownership interest in the property cannot be converted to cash. You tried and failed. (If you actually do sell it, that's even better. Take the cash and run.)

If you own property where you do not live and do not wish to live there, get a local real estate agent and list it.

Do not go into your local SSA office to apply for SSI, tell them about your house and moan and groan about how nobody will buy it—if you've never even tried to sell it.

Ownership

Resources often brings up the issue of legal ownership.

Who owns something is very simple—the person whose name is down as the owner.

Sounds simple, but many people try to complicate it, or ignore it.

If your name is on a car, it's yours. It doesn't matter your daughter paid for it and your son drives it. If your name is on it, it's yours.

Same goes for property. If your name is on it, it's yours. Don't bother telling SSA about how you didn't pay for it. If your name is on it, it's yours.

That's true even if you're so mentally retarded you don't understand the concept of ownership, but your family put property in your name to evade taxes on it.

If your name is on it, it's yours.

This is also true for bank accounts.

If your name is on your adult child's bank account, that money is yours. This can be a BIG problem for SSI recipients. They have their name on somebody else's bank account so their checks can be cashed at the bank or some other reason, but the account is large enough to put them over the SSI limit.

Even if it isn't, every time the other person makes a deposit (perhaps of their bi-weekly paycheck), that money counts as income to the SSI recipient.

Therefore, if your name is on somebody else's account, get it off. If it isn't, keep things that way. Never add your name to somebody else's money or property.

If your name is on somebody's account so you could access the money just in case they died, you can have the bank put your name on with a "POD." POD stands for Proof Of Death. It means that you do not have access to their money without presenting a death certificate.

That means their money is not counted as yours—until they die. Then it does.

Sometimes adult children put mom or dad's name on their account so they can take care of the older/disabled person's business for them.

That's great, but if that person gets SSI, it creates problems.

What you can do instead is set up a joint bank account using the SSI person's money, and keep all the money in the account as the SSI person's. Your name can be on their money to help them out, but you never deposit your personal funds into the account. For your own personal banking, use a separate bank account that does not have the SSI person's name on it.

SSA should have you both sign a statement to this effect.

Life Insurance Policies

Life insurance policies are a common form of resource which CRs have to verify, but the good news is they almost never make someone ineligible for SSI. However, they are the source of a huge amount of work, delayed claims and confusion.

The main form of life insurance is "whole" life insurance. You agree to pay a life insurance companies a monthly premium for twenty years. And when you die, they agree to pay your beneficiary the face value of the policy.

After around 3 years or more, this kind of policy has a cash surrender value. That is how much the life insurance company would pay you if you cashed in the policy. It builds up slowly over time as you continue to make premium payments every month.

Most whole life insurance policies have a table in them which indicates what the cash surrender value is at any given time up to the policy being twenty years old. When it's older than that, SSA must write to the life insurance company.

They also have to write for the cash surrender value of universal or variable life policies, because these values can change over time.

One form of life insurance, term life insurance, does not have a cash surrender value. If that's what you own, tell the CR your policy is term only.

As I mentioned, life insurance is the source of a lot of hassles between SSI people and SSA. Many people do not seem to pay any mental attention to their finances at all.

They tell SSA they own life insurance policies they stopped paying on five years ago. They seem to think term life has a cash surrender value. And that cancer insurance is the same as life. (it's not.)

And you own a life insurance policy if your name is down as the owner even if you are not the insured.

The insured is the person whose life the policy is insuring. The owner is the owner. For adults they are usually the same, but may not be.

If you're the owner of a policy, you're evading the question if you don't tell SSA about policies you own. Sometimes mothers own policies on their children. If Mom's name is down as the owner, she's the owner. (Sometimes it's the child - if you're not sure, consult the policy itself or your agent.)

If you own a life insurance policy and have stopped paying on it, check on its status with the life insurance company. If that policy has a cash surrender value, the company is using that cash surrender value to continue to pay the monthly premiums, and will continue to do so until there is no more cash surrender value left. Then it will cancel the policy.

But until the policy is canceled, it is in effect.

Why don't people who no longer wish to own a certain life insurance policy cancel it themselves and take the cash surrender value out as cash? That's another mystery to me.

And I have no doubt a fair number of life insurance claims are never paid because the dead person's family didn't even realize they had a life insurance policy still in effect, and so don't notify the life insurance company of the death of the insured.

My advice here is—know what life insurance policies you own and what kind of policies they are. If you have any questions, ask your agent. If you don't have them already, get full copies of all those policies. A summary page does not contain the cash surrender value, so sending one in only that delays your claim.

The Burial Exclusion

SSA knows people want to provide for their own burials, so the law contains provisions for that, and this works with life insurance.

(This may surprise those of you in the world of conventional personal finance who believe the purpose of life insurance is to provide for dependents after you die. In the world of SSI recipient finance, the purpose of life insurance is to pay for your own burial. SSI recipients are not supporting themselves, let alone any dependents.)

You are allowed to exclude up to $1,500 to pay for a burial, per person. If you own a life insurance policy on yourself with a cash surrender value of $2,000, the first $1,500 is not a countable resource, only the second $500.

If you own policies on your children, those cash surrender values are excluded up to $1,500 per child.

And if that is not enough for your burial, you can buy a lot. A burial plot of ground is not a countable resource. You can also fund a prepaid burial contract with a funeral so that it's irrevocable. If it's irrevocable, it can't be converted into cash and so is not a countable resource.

If You Have Ownership Interest in an Unprobated Estate

If someone in your family has died, their property may be a resource to you. Maybe they left a will leaving you the property and you haven't enacted the will yet. It does take time, and if it's in process you just have to wait it out. However, most people are letting things like that slide.

Get it done.

Property Essential for Self-Support Exclusion

Some resources produce income. This can include:

Tools or other equipment someone uses to run a business

Land or house that is rented out

Land on which you receive mineral or oil royalties

Property required of an employer for a job (For example, I believe that in some auto dealerships the mechanics own the tools they use.)

There are two requirements for property to be excluded as essential for self-support:

Your net ownership interest must be worth under $6,000.

You must make at least a 6% rate of return.

In practice, this exclusion is little used. There's not a lot of property left you can get an income from with an equity of less than $6,000.

However, if you own a small house in a rough neighborhood you rent out, or you own some tools or musical instruments you use to generate some income, this exclusion is worth mentioning to your CR.

Conditional Payments

What if you do own some property that puts you over the resource limit but you're willing to sell it?

SSA has set up a system where it will pay you conditional payments if you agree to do everything in your power to sell the property. This generally applies to real estate or something else that requires time to sell. It doesn't apply to cash in a bank account which you can simply withdraw any time you wish. But the agency recognizes real estate is not so easy to turn into cash.

You can receive payments for up to 9 months while you try to sell it. This can be extended if necessary. Once you do receive cash for your property, you must refund the conditional payments, so they are like an interest-free loan from the government.

You must make a good-faith effort to sell it. To me that means listing your property with a real estate agent and accepting their advice about what it's worth. It also means accepting the first legitimate offer on the property.

As I write in 2012, the US real estate market is still in a slump because of the financial crisis. However, I also know it's possible to sell property even in this market. One key is not thinking you're going to get a 2007 price.

Transferring Property at Less Than Fair Market Value

The law takes a dim view of people who unload resources to get on SSI.

If you own some property that could keep you off SSI and you decide the heck with putting it on the market by listing it with a real estate agent, you'll just sign a quit claim deed giving it away to a relative...you're asking for bigger problems.

The same applies if you give cash away to get on SSI.

When you apply, you're asked if you've sold or given away any resources in the past three years. If you haven't, just say no.

If you have, you'll be asked for more details.

If you gave $5,000 away to a relative, expect hard questions.

Same if you sold a car. If you put an ad in the paper or sold it to a used car dealer or to your neighbor for what you considered a good price, you're all right. You sold it on the open market.

But if you just gave it away to a family member...you could have a problem, depending on its value.

Basically, if you give away resources to get on SSI, they continue to count as a resource for three years.

Example: Clothilde applies for SSI in March 2011. She says she gave her entire life's savings of $6,000 to her daughter to pay for her wedding in June 2010, so now she has no resources.

If she has no income, SSA will assume if she'd kept that $6,000, she'd have needed to spend the $674 SSI income limit every month (in 2010 and 2011) to meet her needs. That means that by the time she applied for SSI in March 2011, her resources would be below the $2,000 limit anyway, so she is eligible.

Imelda owns some undeveloped land she bought years ago and never did anything with. Before applying for SSI, she signs it over to her daughter. A local real estate agent estimates it could have been sold for at least $30,000. Imelda is not eligible for three years after the close of the property sale. She should have listed the property and sold it for what it was worth, pocketing the net cash.

Maybe some people just want to be nice to their family members. That's touching. But if you're applying for SSI you're asking for help from hardworking taxpayers. They're under no obligation to help out your family, so you're in no position to help your family financially.

Since the "look back" period is three years prior to applying for SSI, it's possible that some of the people who transfer money and property for nothing do so just to be nice.

Planning ahead three years is not a common behavior I've noticed among SSI applicants and recipients.

So all I can say is, you may have to argue that when you made the transfer you had no intention of applying for SSI in the future, and did it for other reasons.

You'll be more credible if you were working at the time you made the transfer, or if your disability had not yet begun.

The CR may or may not believe you. If you are denied and yet believe you did not make the transfer to get on SSI, file an appeal and make your case to the next CR.

My advice is, don't give money or property away even to your family members unless you're sure you're not planning to get SSI in the next 3 years. If you are going on SSI, you can't afford to financially support your family.

Resources are valued as of the first moment of the first day of the month.

Example:

Chris owns 100 shares of the XYZ Company. As of the first moment of May 1, 2011 (a Sunday) the closing stock price was $12 per share. Therefore, for May 2011 those shares are worth $1,200. They will go up and down as the stock market goes up and down, but for SSI purposes, for May 2011 they're worth $1,200. Because that stock is Chris' only resource, he is below the $2,000 limit for May 2011.

By the last stock market close of May 2011, the XYZ Company shares are up to $21 per share. This means Chris' resources for June 2011 are $2,100. He is above the resource limit and therefore not eligible for SSI that month. This is true even if the stock market crashes on June 2 and his shares go back down to $1,200.

Example:

Louise has $5,000 in her savings account as of March 31, 2011. Therefore, as of the first moment of April 1, 2011, that is her balance. She is not eligible for SSI for April 2011.

In April she withdraws $4,000 and prepays her rent, lights, and gas, and stocks her kitchen with canned goods. She reports the change in resources to her local SSA office, giving them her withdrawal slips and receipts to verify she spent the money she withdrew.

Because Louise went below the $2,000 income limit in April, she is eligible for SSI effective May 2011.

Spending Down

As Louise's example (above) shows, SSA can do a separate resource calculation for each calendar month—based on what was owned as of the first moment of the first day of that month.

It's quite possible (and is common) for people to be over the resource and then spend the money to below the $2,000 limit.

According to the law, the money has to be spent—not given away. The law doesn't specify how the money has to be spent.

Some people, such as Louise above, spend it responsibly. Other people...well, if you're a hardworking taxpayer you don't want to know how some SSI recipients spend money.

But if the person satisfies their SSA worker the cash is spent, it is no longer a countable resource as of the first moment of the next month.

Back SSA and SSI benefits are not a countable resource until six months after they're received. I almost never saw anybody who still had that money after two months, let alone six.

SSI Income

Resources are a sort of "threshold" requirement.

Either you're below the resource limit or over it.

If you're over the resource limit, you can't get SSI.

But what if you're below it?

Then SSA must look at your income.

Like resources, most income is countable, but some is not.

Countable income includes:

Wages from working

Net earnings from self-employment

Your share of a TANF grant

Regular cash income from family and friends

In-kind income of food and/or shelter (covered in a separate chapter)

Social Security

Pensions—private, state, military, local and federal

VA pensions

VA compensation

Railroad Board payments

Prizes

Gambling winnings

Royalties

Rental income

Unemployment

Workers compensation

Just about anything that puts cash money into your pocket so you can buy food and shelter

However, most government benefits designed to help poor people do not count as income for SSI because it'd make no sense to give them with one hand and take them away with the other. These include:

Section 8 subsidized rent

Medicaid

Food stamps

Energy Assistance

Natural Disaster Assistance

Refugee Assistance

Earned Income Tax Credits

SSI income also does not include anything which encourages you to be independent. Therefore, countable SSI income does not include:

Scholarships, grants or any help going to school, either academic or vocational

Vocational Rehabilitation or any help training you to get or work a job—even the transportation allowances they give people so they'll attend classes and programs

Sometimes income is declared not countable just because it makes sense to do so. For instance, compensation for being a victim of Nazi atrocities is not countable income.

SSI also does not count as income payments from state and local governments based on need and which do not include federal money. TANF counts as income because it includes federal money, although distributed through the states.

Some states have general assistance or general relief type programs funded entirely by those states and paid based on need.

Borrowing money is not countable income so long as both you and the lender recognize your legal obligation to repay the money.

(Once I spoke with a man who told me his income came from his ex-wife. I questioned him about his obligation to repay. He was quite honest with me: "My ex-wife thinks she's loaning me the money. She wants me to pay her back, and I told her I would. But I'm not going to." Because he did not recognize an obligation to repay his ex-wife, it was not a legal loan and therefore counted as cash income to him, reducing his back SSI check.)

If the lender is a bank or credit card, SSA will assume they want the loan repaid. If the lender is your mother, they'll need to verify it.

Tax refunds are not countable income, because the money comes from paychecks you earned the year before.

Infrequent and Irregular Income

Sometimes people get small amounts of money on an infrequent and irregular basis. If they're very small and unpredictable, this income is excluded. It's just not worth the trouble for SSA to investigate and verify.

Example:

Erin just happens to run into an old school friend—whom Erin hasn't seen in five years—who gives her $10 to buy cigarettes. That's not countable income.

Check Calculations

All right, how does SSA figure out your SSI check based on your income?

It's really not hard.

First we have to make one important distinction: between earned income and unearned income.

Earned income is wages and net earnings from self-employment. You earned it directly. To encourage people to work, earned income is treated differently than unearned income. It cuts your checks a lot less than unearned income.

Unearned income is everything except wages and net earnings from self-employment.

Let's Start with Unearned Income

You get a $20 "general" exclusion.

So if you have unearned income, we subtract $20. Whatever is left reduces your SSI check dollar for dollar.

Example:

Carla receives $450 from Social Security and has no other countable income. In 2011 her monthly SSI benefit is:

450 - 20 = $430 total income

$674 - $430 = $244 SSI check

If you have earned income, SSA counts your gross income. That is, before any deductions for federal, state or local taxes, FICA, or other deductions.

A lot of people get bent out of shape about that. For years they've accepted the federal government takes a chunk of their paychecks by rationalizing it wasn't really "their" money and that's why the government can take it.

So to have SSA count it as "their" money doesn't seem fair to them.

The truth is, it IS your money. The government has the legal right to take it, but they are taking money you earned. It IS your money.

And SSA counts it when you receive it, not when you earn it. Sometimes people get upset because they stop working in May, but don't get their final paycheck until June and then don't think it's fair to reduce their SSI after they've left their job.

But if you think about it for a moment, it'd make even less sense—and would definitely make many people angry—to count money BEFORE it's received. Boy, would SSA get complaints about that!

Once I had a woman who was upset because she was overpaid several years after she stopped working a job. Why? Her former employer was audited, and the auditor discovered they'd never paid her the final paycheck she was due, so the company had to send it to her. And that's when it counted as income to her—when she actually could cash it and spend it on food and shelter.

She was overpaid because she didn't bother to report receiving it, but of course SSA eventually learned about it.

Earned Income

All earned income gets a $65 "earned income" exclusion. That is, SSA doesn't count the first $65 gross you receive in a calendar month. If you made only $65 gross, it would not reduce your SSI at all.

Impairment Related Work Expenses

If you have IRWE as described in the chapter on SGA, that reduces your countable earned income. SSA does start with the total gross as I mentioned, but if you have any expenses directly caused by your disabling condition, your gross is reduced by that before SSA calculates your check.

Example:

Sadie is found disabled due to her MS. She pays a $10 copayment for her MS medicine once a month. Medicaid pays the rest. She goes to work at a job where she has to pay $50 a month for her uniform. Plus she spends $10 a day on lunch. She also pays her brother $5 a day because she is too weak to take the bus. This month she had to pay another $10 copayment for medicine for a Urinary Tract Infection.

Sadie's IRWE is $10 per month she pays for the medicine for her disabled condition. The cost of the medicine for a UTI does not count. The on the job expenses don't count. Every employee has to pay the uniform fee. However, SSA will count the $5 per day transportation charge because it's her physical condition that makes her unable to take the boss. So SSA would have to find out how many days per month she worked, multiply that times 5, then add the $10 to come up with the total IRWE for Sadie.

In June Sadie works 20 days and makes a gross of $1,100.

20 X $5 = $100

100 + 10 = $110 total IRWE for June

1,100 - 100 = $1,000 countable gross income for Sadie for June

Blind Work Expenses

If someone is determined by the state agency to be blind, they are entitled to many more deductions from earned income. The blind can deduct ALL blind expenses and ALL work expenses, even including taxes.

Example: Jose goes to work at the same place as Sadie and has the same general expenses. Plus he had to spend $200 this month to buy a special magnification machine. 35% of his gross pay is deducted from his check for federal, state, local and FICA taxes. He doesn't buy MS medicine but he pays a $10 copay to Medicaid every month for his eye drops.

In June Jose works the same as Sadie and makes the same money.

His BWE are:

$5 per day transportation 5 X 20 = $100

$5 per day lunch 5 X 20 = $100

$50 for his uniform

.35 X 1,100 = $385 for taxes

$10 for eye drops

$200 for the magnification machine

100 + 100 + 50 + 385 + 10 + 200 = $845 total BWE for Jose in June.

Jose's countable earned income is therefore:

1,100 - 845 = $255

You can see that being able to deduct taxes makes a big difference.

All the following examples of calculating earned income assume any IRWE or BWE has already been taken off the top.

You also get the $20 general exclusion. That is used first on unearned income. If you have no unearned income, it's used on your earned income.

So after that $85 is excluded, SSA counts one-half of your total gross.

Example:

Neil's only income is working part-time. This month he receives a gross of $560.

560 - 65 = 495

495- 20 = 475

475 / 2 = $237.50

674 - 237.50 = $436.50 SSI payment amount

But what if Neil also received $200 a month from Social Security benefits?

The $20 general exclusion comes first out of the unearned income. This means it's then not available to be applied to the earned income.

$200 - $20 = $180 countable unearned income

560 - 65 = 495

495 / 2 = $247.50 countable earned income

Total income:

180 + 247.50 = $427.50

674 - 427.50 = $246.50 SSI payment

If you have no countable income, you don't get any exclusions. Your monthly SSI check in 2012 is:

698 - 0 = $698

So for most people, the income calculation is pretty simple. It only gets involved when a lot of paystubs have to be added up.

For couples, the income of both is added together.

Example:

Jewel and Jim Sparling are an eligible SSI couple. Jewel gets $350 Social Security and Jim gets $167 from a private pension.

Their income as a couple:

350 + 167 = $517

They get just one $20 general exclusion:

517 - 20 = $497 countable income as a couple

In 2011 the couple's rate is $1,011 per month:

1011 - 497 = $514 due as a couple

Each of them gets a checks for the same amount:

514 / 2 = $257 each

If Jim were working part-time for $250 a month:

$250 - 65 = 185$

$185 / 2 = 92.50$

$92.50 + 497 = 589.50$ total income for the couple

$1011 - 589.50 = \$421.50$ due as a couple

$421.50 / 2 = \$210.75$ each

Where income calculations get tricky is when the income changes from month to month.

Relationship Between Income and Resources

Income counts the month in which you receive it.

Resources are determined as of the first moment of the first day of the month—effectively, what you owned as of the last moment of the last day of the month before.

Here's how that works out in real life:

Blair Which has no income or resources, so she gets $674 monthly SSI. In April 2011 she wins a radio station prize of $1,000. She is overpaid for her April 1, 2011 SSI check. If she still has any of that $1,000 prize money by the end of April, it can't be over $2,000 so she is under the SSI resource and income limit for May 2011, so she gets that check. (SSA realizes she won't win a prize every month.)

Same situation, only Blair wins $20,000 and has no immediate plans to spend it. She is overpaid for April 2011 for being over the SSI income limit in April 2011. Because she gives the SSA field office the impression she's going to keep most of the cash, they cut off her check effective May 2011. Because she has over $2,000 as of the end of April 2011, she is not eligible for SSI effective May 2011.

In May 2011 she reports taking all her grandchildren to Disneyworld and shows her local SSA field office the receipts and her bank book to verify she now has only $47 left.

As of the first moment of June 2011 she is below the resource limit, so she is eligible for SSI again effective June 2011.

So income is money you receive in this month. Any of the money you still have by the end of the money counts as a resource for the next month.

If someone gives you a countable resource, that counts as income. With cash it's obvious. With other types of resources, it's not.

Example: Helen is on SSI and does not own a car, so her daughter gives her a 2000 Toyota Tercel.

Because a 2000 Toyota Tercel is worth less than $4,500, and it's Helen's only car, it's not a countable resource. Therefore, it is not countable income to Helen.

Instead of a car, Helen's daughter gives her a diamond ring she can sell for $10,000. Helen is charged with receiving $10,000 in income the month she gets the ring, and it will count as a resource which puts her over the resource limit of $2,000 until she sells it and spends the cash below $2,000.

Living Arrangements and In-Kind Support and Maintenance

Closely related to SSI income is the concept of SSI living arrangements.

I've written (effective in 2012), the SSI monthly amount is $698 for most individuals, and that's true.

However, it is not true for people in certain living arrangements.

If you reside an entire month in an institution where Medicaid is expected to pay over half the cost of your care, the most SSI can pay you is $30 for incidental personal expenses.

The most common example of this is when people live in a nursing home. If they are there for long-term care, Medicare does not pay for it. If they can pay for it themselves, they're not going to get SSI anyway.

People who can't afford to pay for nursing homes out of their own money have Medicaid pay for it. If they have no other income, SSI pays $30. If they have income over $50 ($30 plus the $20 general exclusion) they are due no SSI.

Example:

Ricardo gets $450 Social Security and $244 SSI. He is put into a nursing home on a permanent basis March 2011. Medicaid will pay the tab. Therefore, starting with April 2011 he is living throughout the month in an institution where Medicaid is paying over half the cost. Because his Social Security check is over $50, he is cut off SSI.

Example 2:

Lisa gets $674 SSI. On March 16, 2011 she suffers a stroke, goes into an acute care hospital, but before the end of March is admitted into a nursing home for long-term care. Effective April 2011 her SSI amount goes to $30 for her personal expenses while in the nursing home.

On December 20, 2011 she completes her physical rehabilitation program and so the nursing home discharges her back to her own apartment. Therefore, she is due $674 SSI again effective December 2011 (because she did not spend that full calendar month in the nursing home.)

All right, that's the easy one. To be eligible for the full benefit rate of $698 (in 2012), you must be in a living arrangement A or C.

You're in an A if:

You (or your spouse if any) own the house (including ownership interest in an unprobated estate).

You (or your spouse if any) have rental liability.

You buy all your own food separately from other household members (except your own minor children).

You pay your proportionate share of the household shelter bills.

You pay your proportionate share of the household food bill.

You live with only minor children.

Do not live in any one household, but bounce from house to house, park bench to homeless shelter.

Everybody you live with receives income based on need (TANF, SSI, VA pension, Refugee Assistance).

If are in an A living arrangement, your full benefit rate is $698. However, that does not mean you'll get that much, because you may still be receiving in-kind support and maintenance, which counts as income.

Basically, that means you are receiving some form of free food and/or shelter. That does count as income.

Therefore, after asking you questions related to seeing whether you're in an A living arrangement, the CR will ask other questions about receiving free food and/or shelter.

Sharing Computations

When SSA asks a householder for the amount of their average household expenses, they are trying to find out whether or not you are sharing.

After getting the average household expenses, SSA divides by the number of people in the house. That is each person's share. If you're paying that, you're in an A. If you're not, you're in a B.

SSA normally accepts what the householder says their expenses are and how many people live there—sometimes the SSI person doesn't even know—and then just does the math.

If you are living in someone else's household, receive both food and shelter and do not pay your share, you are in a B living arrangement. The benefit rate for a B living arrangement is two-thirds of the A living arrangement benefit rate. (In 2012 that's $465.34.)

In-kind food and shelter can be received from within your household or outside it. That makes no difference to how much it reduces your SSI check. Only the amount of it is important.

Say you live with somebody else and don't pay your proportionate share of their shelter bills. You are receiving inside in-kind income.

Or say you live by yourself, but your mother pays your rent to the landlord every month. That is in-kind income from outside your household.

(NOTE: if your mother gives you the cash for your rent and you take it to the landlord, that is cash income, not in-kind income.

(Therefore, I strongly urge you to receive your food and shelter indirectly, not as cash income.)

Income in the form of free food and/or shelter can take the form of:

Reduced rent

Someone else paying your rent, mortgage, property taxes or utility bills—and that means a direct payment to the provider, NOT cash to you to pay the provider

Someone else buying you food

You live with somebody else and they provide you with food and or shelter (but not both) and you do not pay your proportionate share.

Most living arrangements are fairly simple, but they can get very messy and difficult to sort out.

The whole concept of reducing someone's SSI check because they get free food and/or shelter seems bizarre to some people. But remember the government's intent is to even things out as much as possible.

Is it fair if Joe buys all his own food but Jill is given all her food by her family, Joe and Jill get the same amount of SSI? In that case, Joe would have a financial burden Jill does not. And remember the whole concept of SSI is to provide people's basic needs, which are food and shelter. Jill is not eligible for as much SSI as Joe because she is already getting her food needs met by somebody else.

However, there is a limit to how much SSI will reduce your check based on receiving free food and/or shelter.

That limit is one-third of the full benefit rate plus $20. In 2011, that is $244.66.

For example:

You live alone in an apartment where the rent is $1,000. Your son pays it for you directly to the landlord. You are receiving $1,000 free shelter, but since it is in-kind (your son does not give you the cash), you are charged only the maximum of $244.66, and get a monthly SSI check of $449.34.)

SSA accepts your allegation of owning a house, but if any adults (including children age 18+) live with you, you must verify your rental liability. A lease or rent receipt in your name will do the job.

If you live in somebody else's household, they will have to verify your living arrangements.

For example, it's not uncommon for an SSI claimant to live with a family member or friend, but use their own food stamps to buy their food separately from the others. However, if they are not able to pay the householder for their shelter, they are charged with income for their proportionate share of the shelter bills.

Therefore, SSA will need to talk to the householder to verify you don't get any food from them, and what your share of the shelter bills are, and how much you pay (if anything).

Some householders do not like this, regarding it as an intrusion on their privacy. If your householder refuses to cooperate with SSA, SSA has no choice but to assume you are not paying your share of both food and shelter.

That puts you in a B living arrangement.

When we do ask to talk to your householder, you should explain SSA is trying to decide whether or not you are paying your full proportionate share of food, shelter or both.

Sometimes householders catch a bad case of wishful thinking and want to believe SSA is going to pay their household bills because they're giving someone on SSI a place to stay. Therefore, they exaggerate their household expenses.

This is bad for the person on SSI. That's because the higher the household expenses, the more difficult it will be for the person on SSI to pay their proportionate share.

The math is very simple.

Say there are four people in the household, total, making the SSI person's proportionate share one-fourth.

One-fourth of $900 ($225) is easier to pay than one-fourth of $1400 ($367). But some householders don't seem to understand that.

The math also means if you live with twenty people it'll be a lot easier to pay your proportionate share than if you live with one person.

Your householder should be able to tell SSA their monthly rent or mortgage amount, and average utility bills, and property taxes if their house is paid for.

If they're not sure of these, they can bring in the receipts.

You are not charged with any in-kind income from government programs. It wouldn't make sense for the government to give out a benefit with one hand, then cut your cash income with the other.

Therefore, these government benefits are not SSI countable income although they are in-kind:

Food stamps

Section 8 low income housing (including utility payments they make for their tenants)

Energy Assistance

I realize this is not the easiest concept to understand. Some examples may help:

Melinda lives alone in a Section 8 apartment, gets food stamps, and pays on her light and gas bills only what Energy Assistance provides. Living arrangement A. No countable in-kind income.

Sophie lives with her sister and the sister's children. She receives food and shelter and does not contribute anything toward paying the bills. The sister and her kids are all on TANF. Living arrangement A. Sophie receives no countable in-kind income because everybody she lives with receives needs based income.

Doug lives with his sister and her children. He gets all his food and shelter from his sister who works full-time. Living arrangement B.

Cathy lives with her sister and her 2 children. Cathy alleges buying all her food separately from her sister's family with her food stamps. She does not pay on the shelter bills. The CR would have to verify the separate purchase with the sister, and also the amount of the sister's shelter bills. If the sister agrees she does not provide Cathy with food, Living arrangement A, but the amount of free shelter she receives must be calculated.

Same as above: Cathy's sister's rent, lights and gas total $600. Because $600 / 4 = $150, Cathy is charged with $150 in-kind income.

Same as above, except Cathy's sister's rent, lights and gas total $1,600. $1,600 / 4 = $400 each. $400 is over the current maximum of $265.66, so SSA charges Cathy with the $265.66.

Samantha lives with her 15 year old son. She has no income, so she pays the bills using her son's Social Security check. The household bills total $300. Samantha is in an A living arrangement because it's her household (not the minor child's). She gets $300 / 2 = $150 free food and shelter because her son's Social Security check is his income, not hers.

(A lot of mothers have a lot of trouble understanding the income they get for their children is not supposed to be spent for their own benefit.)

When in-kind income is received from outside the household, SSA also divides that by the number of people.

For example:

Geno rents an apartment for $1,000 and lets four friends stay there with him. His mother pays the rent directly to the landlord. Geno's share is $1,000 / 5 = $200.

Reduced Rent

Although the government allows you to get reduced rent from its Section 8 program, it lowers your SSI check if you get reduced rent from a parent or child.

Example:

Alexa rents an apartment from her daughter and lives in it alone. Her daughter charges all other tenants in the building $500 for the same kind of apartment. But she charges Alexa only $350 because Alexa is her mother. Alexa is charged with $150 in-kind income for the reduced rent.

More on Cash Income Versus In-Kind Income

If you're giving someone $500 cash for them to pay their rent, you may wonder why Social Security counts the total amount as income that reduces their SSI check dollar for dollar—but if you give the money to the landlord instead, that cuts their SSI check only $265.66.

It's the same money out of your pocket, so what's the difference?

Ask any alcoholic, drug addict, gambler or other financially irresponsible person.

They take their food and rent for granted (or just don't care about them). So cash in their hand becomes a temptation many cannot resist.

If the person you're helping does resist temptation and pays the rent responsibly, that's great, but to SSI cash income cuts their check dollar for dollar and in-kind income has a limit.

Therefore, if you're now getting (or giving) cash income to help someone pay such expenses, I strongly advise you to stop immediately.

Pay their landlord directly. Pay their gas, light and water companies directly. Pay their real estate taxes directly to the tax assessor. Pay their property insurance bill directly to the insurance company. Want them to have food? Take them to the supermarket and pay the cashier yourself.

Do not put cash into the hands of an SSI person if you can help it, even if they are responsible. The law is the same for all.

C Living Arrangements

C in this case stands for children.

If a child lives with their parent(s) who have rental liability or ownership interest the child is in a C LA.

If the child lives in someone else's household, they must either pay their proportionate share of the expenses the same as an adult (putting them into an A living arrangement or be in a B living arrangement if they don't pay their share.

In essence, if a child gets food and shelter from their mother and/or father, that's as it should be and their check is not reduced.

However, if the child receives food and shelter from anybody else, that is countable income to them that reduces their SSI check.

Report Living Arrangement Changes Immediately

If you're just applying for SSI, the odds are good you have no income of your own and you're getting by thanks to staying with somebody else, or getting help from them in some way.

It's very common for an SSI applicant to have no income of their own and therefore to be dependent on some family member or friend.

Therefore, depending on the exact circumstances, Social Security puts them in a B living arrangement or charges them with in-kind income.

When people start receiving SSI, it's also common for them to change their living arrangements.

Perhaps they move out into their own place. Perhaps they start paying their proportionate share of the household expenses.

My strong advice is to report such changes immediately. Many people do, but many don't, even though SSA tells them to and it's to their advantage to do so.

Example:

When Sarah applies for SSI she's living with her daughter, who pays all the household bills. When Sarah starts getting SSI, she gets her own apartment and moves out of her daughter's place. She will pay all the bills herself. This means she changes from a B living arrangement to an A living arrangements, and will raise her SSI check from $465.34 to $698.

When Basil applies for SSI he's living with his daughter, who pays all the household expenses. When he starts getting SSI, his daughter demands he pay her $300 a month. He reports this change, the CR talks to his daughter who verifies that is more than Basil's proportionate share of the household expenses. Therefore Basil too goes from a B living arrangement to an A living arrangement, and his check goes from $465.34 to $698.

Three months later, Basil and his daughter move to a new apartment where the rent is much more expensive. Basil's proportionate share of the household expenses is now $870. This is more than he can possibly pay, so he goes back to a B living arrangement, and his check goes back to $465.34 from $698.

You should also report when people move in and out.

Example:

Ethan lives with his sister and his sister's two minor children and pays her $200 a month. This is less than his proportionate share of the household expenses, so he is in a B living arrangement.

In April 2011 his sister's son, the son's girlfriend and their two children move into the household. When the bills are divided by 8 people instead of 4 people, Ethan's $200 covers his proportionate share of the household expenses.

Sally lives with her sister and her sister's two minor children. Sally does not contribute toward paying the bills, but she is in an A living arrangement with no in-kind income because the sister and kids all receive TANF. The sister's son, son's girlfriend and their two children move in, and have no income. Sally now is in a B living arrangement because she does not contribute, and not everybody in the household receives income based on need.

You can get in-kind income from different places. It all counts.

Example:

Paul lives with his sister, who pays all the shelter bills. However, he goes to his mother's house every day and she feeds him. SSA would have to talk to both the sister and the mother to find out how much food and shelter he is receiving.

Loans

It's allowed under SSI law to receive food and/or shelter and owe someone for providing it to you.

However, you must agree with the other person that it's a loan.

You must remain consistent. Don't tell SSA when you first apply you have no loan agreement, but tell them months later that you do, just because your lawyer told you to lie.

And the other person must agree it's a loan.

And if you want to borrow your share of the household expenses, it must be possible for you to pay your share. SSI pays at most $698, so if SSA will not put you into an A living arrangement if your proportionate share of the household expenses is $900. You simply cannot pay that.

In-Kind Income is Subject to Infrequent Income Rules

If someone gives you food and/or shelter on an irregular, infrequent basis—don't even mention it.

Example:

Gail lives with her son who provides her shelter and her day to day food. Once in a blue month an old friend takes her out to lunch. Gail must be charged with the value of the food and shelter from her son, but SSA does not want to hear about the friend taking her out to lunch.

In-kind income boils down to this:

If you are not paying your share of all the food and shelter you receive, you're getting in-kind income unless the help all comes from the government. Or everybody you live with gets income based on need.

Retrospective Monthly Accounting (RMA)

When I started working for SSA a million years ago, SSI income calculations were done on a quarterly basis.

That is, all income you got in a quarter determined how much SSI you were due for each month in that quarter.

When your income was known in advance to SSA and didn't change, this was not a problem.

But many times people's income was not all known to SSA in advance, and did change.

Sometimes people started getting Social Security in the third month of the quarter, making them overpaid for the entire quarter, but they really had not known when the quarter began their Social Security would begin when it did.

So back in early 1982 they switched to a monthly system. However, the fact remained people's income could change faster than SSA could adjust their SSI checks, especially when those checks had already been paid.

Therefore, to avoid accidental overpayments as much as possible, they came up with the Retrospective Monthly Accounting (RMA) system.

If your other income never changes, you will never notice the RMA difference. But sometimes it does, and you may wish to know anyway.

Essentially, SSA pays you SSI based on your income of two months ago.

For example: your May 2011 SSI check is normally based on your March 2011 income.

There are a few exceptions.

If your May 2011 income is over the SSI income limit, you're not due a check for that month, period. You are cut off for any month you are over the income limit.

If you were not eligible for SSI in March 2011, SSA will use your April 2011 income.

It means if you start having new income (such as going to work), your SSI doesn't go down for two months. However, people rarely appreciate this because they don't report going to work as they're supposed to. (SSA has ways of learning about your work, but they take a little time.)

Most people's only other income is Social Security, and once that starts it remains the same, so the main problem this can cause is when people are working and making different amounts of money from month to month.

While they're working, their wages can go up and down, and so will their SSI. If they worked and made a lot of money in March 2011, their May 2011 SSI check will go down a lot even though by May 2011 their wages are also down.

It's almost impossible to avoid overpayments unless people bring their paychecks in every month, early enough for this information to be used by SSA to correctly calculate their monthly benefits.

And that does not prevent SSI amounts from jumping up and down two months after the work hours jump up and down.

And when people stop working, the wages they receive continue to reduce their SSI monthly checks for two months, creating a cash flow problem for them.

Cost of living raises with Social Security, Railroad and VA benefits are coordinated so when those checks go up because of a COLA, the new amounts are automatically used by SSI. You get an SSI COLA increase at the same time. SSA and the other agencies handle this automatically.

My advice is to follow SSA instructions and report any and all changes in your income—up or down—immediately. Go into your local field office or call the 800 number. Eventually I'm sure they'll be able to take these reports online.

Keep all documentation to verify the income, and do make a note of when you report the change. Keep track of the date, time, whether you called or went into the office, and the name of the representative you spoke with.

If you go to work, know when you started, the name of your employer, your hourly wage, how many hours a week you expect to work, and your payment schedule (every other Friday beginning May 6, or whatever). That's what SSA needs to know to accurately estimate your wages.

Then keep all your paystubs and take them into your local office after you've received the last one for each month.

If you have some unexpected income, such as receiving an inheritance or a prize, report it right away. Bring in the documentation.

SSI Marital Status

One thing that affects SSI eligibility a lot is whether or not they are married and living with their husband or wife.

If so, other issues come into play depending on the situation.

From the standpoint of receiving SSI, living with a spouse does nothing good for you.

If your spouse is 65 or over, disabled or blind and meet the other criteria, they should either already be on SSI or applying for it with you.

If you are both eligible for SSI, you receive SSI at the couple's rate.

The couple's rate is one and a half times the individual rate, NOT double the individual rate.

If your spouse has income but it's not based on need, their income count as yours, reducing your benefit amount, sometimes to zero. If they own enough money or property, their resources can prevent you from being eligible for SSI.

It's amazing how many couples took a vow to love, honor and cherish each other... until they can get a government check.

And it's amazing how many times a couple will come into the SSA office because one member wants SSI disability, but the other one is working and making enough money to prevent the disabled spouse from getting SSI. After everything is explained to them, they are suddenly "separated"—without moving a muscle!

Legally Married Spouses at the Same Address Live Together

So the issue of marital status can be important, and therefore is a source of many disputes.

If you live at the same address as your legal spouse, you live together.

Period.

That includes living in the same apartment, same boarding house room, same house, and same mobile home.

If you have separate apartments in the same apartment house, separate rooms in the same boarding house, separate flats in the same four-family flat, or separate rooms in the same nursing home, then you are separated.

By the way, SSA does not care whether you're sleeping together or not. Plenty of people have sex without being married, and plenty of married people don't have sex.

If you're at the exact same address you're counted as a couple. If you don't like that, separate for real.

Holding Out

The original SSI law was passed in 1972. If you were born after that year, you probably think romantic couples in the United States have always lived together openly before getting married (or just to live together).

Nothing could be further from the truth.

Prior to the social upheaval of the late 1960s, men and women did NOT live together prior to marriage. Even if they could have found a landlord to rent to them, it would have been a scandal even in the most socially tolerant neighborhoods.

By 1972 many young men and women were doing so, but it was still controversial and something to hide from your parents (or shock them with).

What did happen in some cases is men and women lived together without getting married for various reasons (often because one or both had a separated spouse and nobody wanted to pay a lawyer for a divorce, which was a lot harder to get in those days), so they lived together without being actually married, but hid that by telling everybody they were married.

So part of the original SSI law is the concept of marriage by "holding out."

If you are living with a unrelated person of the opposite sex and apply for SSI, the CR should ask you whether you and that person are "holding yourselves out to the community as being husband and wife."

That includes telling friends and family you're married even though you're legally not. Or introducing that person as your husband/wife. If the woman uses the man's name. If you tell your landlord you're married. If you have your names on each other's bank accounts, especially with the woman using the man's last name.

If you and that person are not presenting yourself to family or friends as being married, just clearly say so.

Many times people told me they're engaged (which means they plan to get married but haven't yet done so) or just boyfriend or girlfriend—or have no romantic relationship at all.

Barring any evidence to the contrary, that should all be acceptable to the CR.

And if you and the man/woman are not holding out, then don't come into the SSA office and start telling CRs you're married. (Yes, people do that—and then wonder why we treat the other person as their spouse. They forced it.)

If you and the other person ARE holding out, in the eyes of SSA for SSI purposes you are just as much married as if you are legally married.

That means you can both go on SSI as an eligible couple, or the other person's income and resources can affect your eligibility.

Therefore, my advice is if you're living together with a person of the opposite sex, don't call yourselves married—to anybody—unless you really are.

In this day and age, it makes no sense unless you're trying to game the SSI system.

Once I interviewed a woman who had been married to a man who had a good job. She had a child by another man on SSI who was fathered by another man, and the stepfather's income was high enough to prevent the child from getting SSI.

So, being a couple very much in love, they got divorced so the child could get an SSI check (they believed).

Only they continued living together and telling all their friends and family they were married. She was still on his health insurance on work (I wonder what that insurance company thought about paying medical claims for a divorced wife). People who knew about the divorce thought they'd gotten remarried.

It was a very clear case of holding out.

Which meant the stepfather's income still made the child ineligible for SSI, so the mother got angry with me.

They got divorced only to put the child on SSI and then were shocked to learn they couldn't scam the system that easily.

Report All Marital Status Changes

People on SSI are required to report all changes in their marital status.

If you're single when you get on SSI but later get married and start living with your spouse, report that.

If you're living with a spouse when you get on SSI and later separate, report that.

Closely related to the concept of SSI marriage is deeming.

Deeming of Income and Resources

I've touched on this, but I'll try to make it more clear.

The SSI law assumes people in certain relationships have a legal obligation to help each other.

This includes spouses living together; parents living with children and sponsors of aliens (who are indeed legally responsible, because they did promise to support the alien when they were seeking to enter the United States).

This means if you're living with a spouse (through legal marriage or holding out), and that person has income, they're obligated to help you.

Therefore, SSA will count some of their income and resources as yours, and that is included as your resources when SSA is deciding whether you're eligible for a check. Part of their income is counted as yours when deciding how much you're eligible for.

What if—as is extremely common—the SSI partner claims their spouse doesn't give them any cash?

Makes no difference. SSA is a not a marriage counseling service or a personal financial adviser. No sane CR tries to do anything but pay the person correctly. How couples divvy up their funds together is a private matter.

What if a wealthy movie star married a homeless person with no income or resources? Would it be fair to pay that spouse taxpayer money just because they claim their movie star spouse gives them no cash—but they're living in a mansion in Beverly Hills with plenty of food and a swimming pool?

No.

So all I can say is, SSA must treat all couples the same. If you don't like how much cash your spouse gives to you, you must talk to your spouse. It's not SSA's business. See a marriage counselor of you wish. Or separate if you wish (which means actually separating, not remaining in the same household), and then report it to SSA.

The same goes for parents (yes, even including stepparents) and the children.

Although many parents seem to think the responsibility for financially supporting their children is primarily on the government, SSA puts it on parents the children live with—yes, including stepparents, as shocking and surprising as that is to many people. It doesn't matter the man is not the biological father of the children. When he marries their mother, her children become his financial responsibility as well.

Men, if you don't like that, don't marry a woman with children you didn't father.

Anyway, counting a spouse's income toward calculating your SSI and counting one or two parents' income toward calculating a child's SSI is known as deeming.

Some of the spouse or parent's income is deemed to belong to the SSI spouse or child.

It can also be both, because there are families where one spouse works, the other spouse is on SSI and they have one or more children on SSI.

In that case, the working spouse/parent's income is first deemed to the SSI parent/spouse. Nothing is deemed to children unless there's enough income to make the SSI parent/spouse over the SSI income limit.

When there is more than one child, the deemed income is split between them equally.

SSA also takes into account any children in the household that must be supported who are not on SSI.

If someone gets some kind of income based on need, such as ADFC, a VA pension or SSI, then their income is not deemable.

Deeming calculations are not for the faint of heart.

I don't recommend them as a do-it-yourself project. I used to do them with a piece of paper and a pen, but the paper was a special form with complete instructions. And now the agency wants CRs to use a computer program.

Go into your nearest Social Security field office and they'll do it for you, and take the child's claim if warranted.

If you and/or a spouse make a significant amount of income, don't be surprised if your child is not eligible.

SSI is meant to support children who otherwise wouldn't have enough food or shelter. It's NOT a reward for everyone who has a disabled child.

There are many hardworking parents who make too much money for their disabled child to get SSI, but who are still struggling. And they pay taxes to support SSI.

Being over the SSI income limit does not mean you are rich. Government welfare programs are not for everyone who is not rich. It doesn't even mean you're financially comfortable. It's not supposed to. It just means you're able to provide your child with food and shelter without government aid.

The same applies to those of you with a disabled spouse who can't get on SSI because your income is too high.

Being over the SSI income limit does not mean you're rich, not by a long shot. But it means you can afford to provide the basics so your husband or wife doesn't starve in the street.

My job with this book is to tell it the way it is. If you don't like the way it is, write your Congressman. I had no power to change anything when I was an SSA employee, and even less power now.

Besides, if you think not starving in the street is not an accomplishment, try visiting one of the many countries in this world where people (including children) do starve in the streets—and be grateful you can take not starving in the street for granted. Not everyone in this world is so lucky.

Filing for Other Benefits

SSI is intended to be the income of last resort. It's what you get when you don't have enough other money to live on.

Consequently, one of its requirements is you must file for any other benefits you may be eligible for.

This seems like a beneficial requirement. Just go and apply for other benefits you may not have known about, which may be more money than SSI.

The most common other benefit is Social Security. When someone comes into an SSA office to apply for either SSI or Social Security, they're automatically screened for both.

The most common referral to another agency is to the Veteran's Administration. If you're a veteran, you served at least 90 days active duty during a wartime period, don't have an unfavorable discharge, you are now disabled and need the money you may qualify for a VA pension. Take your discharge paperwork to your local Veteran's Administration office.

Think about places you've worked in the past that were covered by pension plans, whether through the employer or the union. If you worked there a significant period (a few months won't cut any mustard), check out the Human Resources Department or the benefits office of the union you belonged to.

Check it out if you ever worked years for the United States federal government, a state or local government.

The worst that can happen is they tell you no.

1619(b)

SSI recipients who rely on Medicaid to pay their medical bills can generally continue to remain on Medicaid even while they are working and making so much per month they are not eligible to receive SSI checks.

This is addressed by Section 1619(b) of the SSI law.

Therefore, somebody who used to get SSI but is cut off due to earnings can remain on Medicaid indefinitely. If they lose their job, they can go right back on SSI after a review to update their information.

The one catch is wages must be the ONLY reason you are not receiving SSI for Section 1619(b) apply.

Example:

Christy was on SSI until May 2009 when she got a job paying $2,000 per month. She informed SSA and her local Medicaid agency right away.

Her SSI checks stopped, but she continued to use Medicaid to pay for her doctor visits and her medications.

In May 2011 she was laid off from her job. She took the letter from the company into her SSA office. They completed a review and resumed her SSI checks.

Example:

Same situation, only this time Christy was laid off her job in May 2010 and she begins collecting $250 a week in employment benefits.

In June 2011 her unemployment benefits run out, so she goes to SSA to resume her SSI.

However, because she was over the income limit for a year for a non-wage source of income (unemployment), she is not eligible for Section 1619(b).

She must file a new application and get a new disability medical decision.

Other Useful Work Incentive Programs

Plans for Achieving Self-Support—PASS Plans

Social Security has a variety of legal technicalities which are called "work incentives." They are not well understood or widely used.

I described one of them, Section 1619(b) which allows people not getting SSI due to returning to work the right to keep Medicaid and to go right back on SSI if their work stops in the last chapter.

One for SSI recipients I always thought was a good idea, but can remember only one person ever using all the way, is called a Plan for Achieving Self-Support.

There are a many SSI recipients who could work if they had some marketable job skills. If they could get the proper education and/or job training to acquire those skills, they could get a job in that field.

However, that education and training costs money, which SSI recipients don't have.

With a PASS plan, however, the SSI recipient is allowed to earn and save the required money without reducing the checks they use to pay their basic living expenses.

Example:

Tim learns from a vocational counselor he could perform the duties of a pharmacy technician. To qualify, however, he has to go to pharmacy tech school for a year. The tuition including books and all fees is $5,000.

He is working at McDonald's, which is reducing his SSI check. He proposes to SSA, and they accept, that he be allowed to work at McDonalds without having his SSI check reduced by his wages. He puts all his wages into a separate bank account until he has enough to pay his tuition to pharmacy school. After a few months he has over $2,000 saved, but SSA waives the usual resource limit because it's money he's saving to pay his pharmacy tech tuition. He uses his full SSI check to pay his ordinary living expenses of food and shelter.

When he can pay his tuition, he does so, and begins attending classes.

A year later he is a certified pharmacy tech and gets hired by a local drug store and goes off SSI.

Example:

Mark comes into his SSA office saying he wants a PASS plan to start his video production business. He's already invested $5,000 in video equipment he bought last year with his back SSI check.

Mark's request is denied. He already owns the video equipment. Nobody's stopping him from using it for a business if he wishes. He did not get prior approval for his PASS plan. Besides, he's had the video equipment for a year and failed to do anything with it (except let his family watch movies), so his sincerity is questionable.

Example:

Martin comes into the SSA office and requests approval for a PASS plan to take classes to get his Microsoft Certified Systems Engineer (MCSE) so he can get a job working on computer networks.

Martin's request is denied because his IQ is only 78. Therefore it's extremely unlikely he could complete and pass the schooling necessary for the MCSE certification, which is highly technical.

Ticket to Work

This is a program that began in the early 2000s, and is intended to encourage more disability recipients to return to work.

Generally, you must have been getting disability benefits for at least three years.

People on disability get a "ticket to work" which entitles them to vocational services from an agency that is an expert.

They also get other incentives.

Medicare and Medicaid eligibility are extended.

They do not undergo CDRs.

I don't have overall statistics. Participation in my experience was almost nil.

However, once you've been on disability for at least 3 years, if you haven't already received a ticket in the mail, call up SSA or come in to request one.

Redeterminations

SSI is income based on your need for it. That is evaluated, as I've explained, mainly on your income, resources and living arrangements.

Those are all items which can—and often do—change.

Therefore, the government has the legal right to perform reviews every so often to determine whether or not you are still eligible for benefits, and if so, whether you're due the amount you're getting—or a higher or lower amount.

These reviews are called redeterminations.

Many years ago, the agency tried to perform full redeterminations on everybody once a year. However, that's an ideal long forgotten because of staffing shortages.

They began sending out short form questionnaires (SSA-8202) to many recipients, and accept their answers on the form unless there's reason to doubt them.

And many people are reviewed only once every three years, or less.

However, the agency does determine which recipients are most likely to have a change, and therefore those who need redeterminations more often.

Those people are then contacted by mail or telephone or asked to come into the office, and a full interview is conducted, and full SSA-8200.

If the SSI recipient has a spouse or is a child living with one or both parents, an SSA-8010 is completed on those deemors.

If you're 90 years old, haven't changed your address in 20 years and you have no other income—or your other income is something stable, such as Social Security—you will probably have redeterminations done very rarely.

If you're disabled, you have wages on your record, you have in-kind income on your record, and you have a spouse who is working, you can expect frequent redeterminations.

That doesn't mean elderly people don't sometimes have a change that makes them overpaid (I've done redeterminations on elderly people who got married, for example, and didn't report it).

However, it means certain records are more likely than others to have unreported changes, and therefore more worth the time and attention of SSA's overworked CRs.

Sometimes people don't like to answer the questions, regarding them as an intrusion on their privacy by the government.

This has to do with SSI, which is based on your need for it. When you accept what's essentially a form of welfare, you are voluntarily giving up some of your privacy. The government has the legal obligation to make sure it's paying people correctly.

If SSA simply accepted people's word, everybody in the country (who's willing to lie) would be on SSI.

So SSA does have the right to ask you questions, request evidence and documentation from you, and to get information from you from other databases.

If you don't like this, you do have the right to refuse to cooperate. In which case, SSA has the right (actually, it's a legal obligation), not to pay you.

And one reason for SSA not devoting as much man and woman power to conducting these redeterminations, is their ability to detect unreported income and resources has greatly increased in the past 30 years.

As I mentioned, SSA gets information from other sources. It informs you of that when you first apply. Nobody tells you the full extent to which SSA can get information on you, and in my experience claimants at that point do not absorb the information and think through the consequences, but you are informed.

Let me give you a clue: the world is full of things called computers. Computers not only enable people to talk to each other across great distances, the computers can talk to each other, trading information.

If you get have any of the following and don't report it to SSA, you'll eventually be caught. Maybe not tomorrow, but eventually:

Unemployment

Wages

Pensions

Workers Compensation

VA benefits

Bank Accounts

Inheritances

Life insurance payments

Prizes

Gambling winnings

Royalties

Net Earnings from Self-Employment

Stocks

Certificates of Deposit

Savings Bonds

Mutual Funds

If you have any of these and haven't reported it, I suggest you call 1-800-772-1213 or go into your local field office with all documentation. Take in all your paystubs, your stock certificates, your certificates of deposit or whatever it is.

The sooner you report, the better you look and the less you'll be overpaid. And even if you're reporting late, that's better than SSA finding out first from a computer alert on you.

This is not related to SSA, but it's a similar example. I knew a woman who was working, but who went into her local unemployment office and falsely reported she'd been laid off. She collected weekly unemployment checks for several months.

But the state unemployment agency that pays those checks is the very same agency that receives quarterly reports of earnings from employers.

Her employer obviously continued to report her wages, and the state unemployment agency was "miraculously" able to put two and two together and realize she was not due her weekly unemployment checks.

The judge sentenced her to community service, so she was lucky.

And I have no idea how she thought she could get away with that.

Many SSI recipients—including people who KNOW they're getting checks for having low IQs—somehow think they're smart enough to fool SSA.

They didn't bother to listen when informed SSA could get information on them from other agencies, and then they're surprised when we eventually learn about the night they hit the jackpot at the local casino. And are amazed SSA makes them overpaid for that month, and denies their waiver request because they didn't report it themselves.

If You Get SSI, You Can't Afford to Help Your Friends Evade Their Income Taxes

When it comes to SSI recipients winning at some form of racetrack or casino gambling, it's simply amazing how many claim it wasn't they who won, but their friend who asked them to pick up their winnings for them.

First of all, I believe most of the time that story was a total lie. It was the SSI recipient who bet on the winning horse and who won the slots jackpot, and that's why the winnings are in their name and Social Security number.

If it was ever not a lie, I believe they were still paid some money by the friend to put the friend's winnings in their name and Social Security number.

And by doing so, they were conspiring with their friend to help the friend evade income taxes, which is a federal felony, and so these people are lucky SSA does not report all of them to the IRS for criminal investigation and fraud. They might be doing so now, for all I know.

In any case, if the money was claimed under your name and Social Security number (and SSA workers know you have to present ID, so nobody did this behind your back), it's your income. And therefore you are overpaid for that month, and you will be the one to have to pay back the overpayment.

My advice is if you go to a casino, you confine your activity to watching other people gamble, or listening to the bar band who were superstars 30 years ago.

If you can afford to gamble, you don't need SSI.

After all, supposedly you need your entire check to support yourself. So how can you afford to support your local casinos with taxpayer money?

That's if you lose. If you win, you're over the SSI limit and overpaid.

So either you lose the money taxpayers worked hard for so you don't have to starve on the streets, or you win and lose your SSI. You lose either way.

In my opinion, people on any kind of welfare should not be allowed to gamble, but I understand enforcing such a law would be difficult. And states with lotteries would object to it the most, because they know a lot of their lottery customers are welfare recipients. It's a way the states have of getting some of the welfare benefits they pay out back into the state's treasury.

Anyway, if your income, resources and living arrangements change, do report that right away.

In some cases, the CR may complete a full redetermination on you based on your report.

They may only put in the change.

Many people assume any change is for the worse, and so they are afraid of reporting changes for fear their check will be cut.

In some cases, that's a valid fear. Some changes do indeed reduce your check amount. However, it's still better to honest, because you'll be caught sooner or later, and will have a huge overpayment plus penalties.

However, in many cases people mess themselves up by not reporting changes. I've seen people due large amounts of back money thanks to a redetermination. And I've seen cases where they lost money because they waited so long to report beneficial changes.

So, you must recognize if you receive SSI you (and any deemors) are subject to periodic reviews. Just answer the questions and provide the necessary evidence.

However, just as with CDRs, you don't have to go looking for a redetermination. When SSA wants to do one on you, it will contact you.

If they want to do one with by mail, they'll mail you the self-help SSA-8202. Take the time to read the questions carefully. They're not hard, and they're not designed to be tricky. But many times people have to be recontacted because they didn't understand what they were checking off.

And know or learn how to write numbers, and where to put the decimal. I can't tell you how many time somebody has written something like "22500" for how much they had in the bank, when they really meant "225.00." That missing decimal point makes all the difference to your eligibility for SSI.

If you need help, get it. If you don't have family or friends to help you, take it into your local office.

If you don't return the form at all, then you are asking to have your check stopped. It is not voluntary. It's a requirement to get future checks.

If you are called by a CR, answer the questions. If you are suspicious, make an appointment to be called, or go into your local office.

If they make an appointment for you, keep it if at all possible. If not, go at another time.

But don't ignore it, if you want to continue receiving SSI.

They do have the authority to suspend your check if you don't cooperate, and will do so.

Until you hear from SSA, your only obligation is to report changes. If there are no changes to report, take it easy.

Overpayments

If you do get approved for benefits from Social Security, you may at some point in the future receive a notice of overpayment.

They happen.

Don't freak out or panic.

They happen for good reasons and bad. It can be your fault, Social Security's fault or nobody's fault.

Because Some Social Security Beneficiaries are Dependents, They Can Be Overpaid Because of the Wage Earner

Let's say you are receiving wife's benefits on the record of a man getting Social Security DIB. He goes back to work and works long enough, and makes enough money, to prove he is no longer disabled, but it takes time for Social Security to learn of this, because he doesn't report it as he's supposed to.

Because you get Social Security on his record, you're also overpaid. Maybe you knew he was back to work and maybe you didn't. Maybe he told you he reported his work to SSA and maybe he didn't. But you are still overpaid.

Don't take it personally. A notice of overpayment is not a letter meant to "blame" you or judge you. Their language is factual in tone and content.

A lot of people get angry with Social Security over such situations. My advice is to save your anger for the person who actually caused the overpayment. And for yourself if you knew they were doing something you were supposed to report, but you didn't report it.

The agency does make a great effort to prevent overpayments by stressing to people their reporting responsibilities over and over again. Many times, people don't listen. Then there's a change they should report, but they don't, and so they get overpaid when SSA learns the truth.

Sometimes people report the change and still get overpaid. That can happen because of computer timing issues. It can also happen because the agency is understaffed and cannot do everything it should as quickly as it should.

However, you should not think that lets you off the hook for failing to report a change. Or to return money or checks you know you're not eligible for.

If you're on Social Security disability, the main cause of overpayments is you returning to work and failing to report it. And an investigation shows your work is enough to prove you are no longer disabled.

If you're retired, the most common cause of overpayments is taking early retirement, but failing to report your work, or earning more in the year than you reported you would.

Disabled adult children can be overpaid for getting married and failing to report it (if they marry they are no longer "children" no matter how disabled, and so not eligible.)

If you're on SSI, you can get overpaid in numerous ways. Receiving income you fail to report is the biggest one.

Liability for Overpayments

The person to whom the checks belong to is the person liable for the overpayment.

For most people, this is obvious.

Some people have representative payees who get their checks and spend the money for them. However, the representative payees are not personally liable for an overpayment so long as they use the money properly for the actual beneficiary.

This also includes people getting checks for children.

It's quite common for children to be overpaid, especially on SSI. Obviously the kids don't know or understand what's going on, but they're still liable.

Some SSI children have mothers who love to cause large overpayments.

If You Are Still Receiving Monthly Benefits

If you are still receiving checks, your overpayment notice will inform you that starting with the month two full months after the date of the overpayment notice, SSA will began withholding 100% of your monthly benefit for you to begin repayment of the overpayment.

If you're on SSI, they'll propose withholding 10% of the full benefit amount—as of 2012 $69.80 for individuals and $52.40 for each member of a couple.

The main exception is if the amount of the overpayment is smaller than your monthly benefit, SSA will withhold only what you are actually overpaid.

Another exception is that if you are "dually entitled." That means you're getting Social Security on two different records. Perhaps you're overpaid on your husband's record but also receive on your own record. The amount you get off your husband's record can be withheld, but not what you get on your own record.

If you agree to the proposed withholding out of your checks, you don't need to do anything. It will happen automatically.

If you believe the overpayment was not your fault, you have the right to file for a waiver.

A waiver is a request to SSA not to have to pay the money back.

For SSA to approve a waiver, it must find you meet two requirements:

1. You are not at fault in creating the overpayment.

2. You cannot afford to pay back the overpayment.

Notice you must meet BOTH requirements. If the CR who takes your waiver request decides you are at fault, you must repay the overpayment.

You can file for a waiver using form SSA-632:

http://www.ssa.gov/online/ssa-632.pdf

The first three pages collect information on whether or not you're at fault. The other pages go exhaustively through your financial status.

If you get Social Security checks, you must complete all those pages asking you about you and any spouse's income and resources, and what your average monthly expenses are.

If you are receiving SSI, the agency assumes you cannot afford to pay the money back. That doesn't mean you're off the hook, though. You must still prove the overpayment was not your fault. If you did not report the change that made your overpaid, you will probably have to pay the money back.

The decision about whether or not you're at fault is made by the CR who receives or completes your SSA-632, so it's a good idea to be nice to them. Their decision should cover the facts of the case. However, CRs can write up their decision to support a finding either of fault or no fault.

In general, if you fail to report a change, your chances of getting a waiver approved are slim.

You must remember this. SSI employees, especially CRs, spend a lot of time informing people of their reporting responsibilities.

A lot of time.

They want you to understand what affects your check.

When you first apply for benefits and the requirements are new to you, I'm sure it's difficult to understand everything you're told.

That's why SSA gives everyone claims receipts with their reporting responsibilities printed on them.

If you didn't understand everything you were told—and this is understandable, though through reading this book you've now got a head start on the general public—you're expected to read the reporting responsibilities when you get home.

And keep them where you can look them over later, if something happens which you're not sure about.

Yet, the truth is, many people fail to report important changes.

Sometimes it's a deliberate effort to conceal from SSA a change they believe would stop, reduce or prevent their checks.

Often it's just a plain reluctance to cooperate with the government even when asking the taxpayers for money.

Many times the change would reduce or stop their checks—but many times people fail to report changes that would increase their checks.

A strange fact, but true. If I had a dollar for every time I felt like I was forcing an SSI person to accept a higher benefit—because they were reluctant to tell me about changes that meant they were due more money—I'd be lying in the sun of a tropical beach instead of writing this book.

Anyway, experienced CRs are the least likely to approve a waiver if you didn't report the change, because by the 10,000th time you explain the responsibilities, you want people to listen to you.

The amount of the overpayment has an effect also. Although circumstances can vary, the higher your overpayment, the longer something was going on SSA didn't know about it, and the worse you look.

It's much easier to get a $800 overpayment waived than a $23,000 overpayment.

If You Cash Two Checks for the Same Month, Forget the Waiver

Some recipients learn SSA is such a nice government agency if they call up three days after their check was supposed to be received and report it was not received, SSA will send them a replacement check automatically—without verifying they didn't get the original check.

Some recipients think that's such a nifty way to receive extra money, they repeat it for months in a row.

Until the Treasury Department informs the Social Security Administration they believe the same person cashed both checks for the same month.

Then you get an overpayment notice for all the checks you double cashed.

Your chances of getting a waiver approved for cashing two checks for the same month are close to zero.

And in that case, the agency will withhold your entire monthly check to repay the overpayment, even if you're on SSI.

If you double negotiate three checks in a row, your checks can be stopped for three months.

And if the Treasury Department believes you're abusive enough, they can try to get you convicted of fraud (a federal felony). And sometimes they succeed.

And if, later on, your check actually is lost or stolen in the mail, you don't receive a replacement automatically, but must wait for the Treasury Department to investigate.

In the interest of helping people who actually don't receive their checks (they do get lost in the mail and stolen), SSA will believe you—until you prove you're dishonest. Then you're not believed, just like the boy who cried wolf.

Even if SSA believes the overpayment is not your fault, it won't approve the overpayment if you can afford to pay it back.

SSA assumes SSI recipients cannot afford to repay, so to get a waiver approved, SSI recipients just have to prove they were not at fault.

If you get Social Security benefits of any kind, however, there is no such presumption, because it is not income based on need.

You can file the same SSA-632 form to request not a waiver, but that Social Security withhold only some money from your monthly checks, not 100%.

If your monthly check is high enough to pay your monthly bills and still have some money left over, SSA will likely decide you can afford to make some kind of monthly payment even if it's not the original 100% proposed.

If you can afford to pay $10 per month, they may have you pay that $10 even if it's going to take 20 years before the overpayment is fully paid off.

You will have to convince the CR your expenses are accurate and necessary.

Back in the 1980s I took a waiver request on someone who told me their monthly cable bill was $60 a month. That was back when cable was not in every house, basic service was about $10 per month and Internet and long distance phone services were not included. It may not sound like much now over twenty years later, but in those days that was a lot of money to spend just on TV—far more than even the average cable TV customer did. $60 meant they had every movie channel and several extra TVs.

I decided if they could afford to pay so much to the local cable TV company, they could afford to pay something every month on their SSI overpayment.

Your CR may not be as mean as I was—or may be meaner.

If You're Now Getting A Different SSA Benefit

Sometimes people get overpaid on SSI but they're now getting Social Security, or vice versa.

In years past, people used to go on SSI because they hadn't worked enough to be insured for Social Security. Then they'd go to work and rack up large overpayments on SSI for years, and then "escape" by going on Social Security (because they'd worked enough to be insured) and were eligible for a monthly DIB check higher than the SSI income limit.

However, the government finally wised up to this, and now will take your SSI overpayments from your Social Security checks and vice versa.

SSI Penalties

If you are a currently receiving SSI checks and you did not report the change that created the overpayment, you can be charged a penalty in addition to the original amount of the overpayment.

The first time penalty is $25, second time penalty $50, and the third plus penalty amount is $100.

Sometimes people take a very short view, because SSA withholds only the $25 in one month, and that's now less than the usual 10% of the full benefit amount of $69.80 (as of 2012). Even the $50 penalty is now less than $69.80.

But if they keep refusing to report changes, they can start having $100 penalties deducted from their SSI check.

If You No Longer Receive a Monthly Benefit Check

Social Security will send you an overpayment notice that requests you refund the overpayment.

You still have the right to file for a waiver.

If you can't refund the entire amount at once, SSA will generally accept a monthly refund plan. Let them know how much you can afford to refund every month. There's usually no problem if your plan will refund the entire overpayment within 3 years.

If it will take over 3 years, SSA should complete the financial pages of an SSA-632 to verify you cannot make larger monthly payments.

However, when all is said and done, when push comes to shove, SSA will accept any refund you make.

I advise you to pay something, because SSA has other ways to collect if you don't pay voluntarily.

SSA now has the capacity to go after you much like Visa or a finance company might if you owe them money. If they can document you have some income (a good job for example), they'll go to court and try to get money withheld from your paychecks.

Your unpaid debt to Social Security is also reported to the major credit bureaus, so someday you may find your application for a Visa card or a home mortgage denied because you have a debt to SSA you're not making payments on, lowering your credit score.

They will also withhold overpayments from your tax refunds.

I guarantee that every January and February there are many unhappy young adults who are expecting to receive large tax refunds to party on, just like their friends and co-workers receive, but who instead get a letter from the IRS notifying them that their tax refund is being withheld to go toward paying off their SSI overpayment.

They go into their local SSA office and complain but there's little they can do. They can file for a waiver but unless they can prove their mother (or other payee) was not at fault in creating the overpayment, it will be denied.

Obviously they were not at fault themselves. They were children when the overpayment happened. But they're liable for the overpayments their mothers created. The mothers probably had waivers denied years ago.

My advice is to tell your mother (or other payee) to refund the overpayment they caused.

You may be able to get Social Security and SSI overpayments discharged through bankruptcy. For that, you must see a lawyer.

If all else fails, your overpayment will sit on your record until you retire. Unless you die first, SSA knows that sooner or later you'll be back to file for RIB at age 62 or above or for SSI aged benefits at age 65.

Then, long after you think the overpayment is over and forgotten, it will be collected from checks in your old age.

If you believe the overpayment notice is not correct, you can file for a reconsideration.

Take this course only if you believe SSA has the facts of your case wrong or has misapplied the law.

You should not file a reconsideration just because you "hope" SSA has its facts wrong or misapplied the law. I'm not saying SSA is never wrong. It certainly can be. And if you know it's wrong (NOT guessing or hoping), then of course file for a reconsideration.

Example:

Joe receives SSI and gets a notice he is overpaid due to work. This puzzles him because he really has not worked. He calls up SSA and is told the employer is Taco Bell. He files a reconsideration and reports his brother, Joey, whose Social Security number is just one digit different and who also gets SSI, works for Taco Bell. The CR talks to Taco Bell and verifies the worker is really Joey, who may be fired for giving Taco Bell his brother's Social Security card when he was hired. So Joe wins his case. The wages are removed from his SSI record, eliminating his overpayment. They are added to Joey's SSI record, making him overpaid instead.

Joey is then referred for a fraud investigation because he knowingly tried to hide his wages from Social Security.

Example:

Charice gets an overpayment notice she's overpaid $1985 due to working for Burger King from April 2010 through January 2011. She goes into the Social Security to complain. She files a reconsideration because she insists, although she did work for Burger King during that period, she didn't make "that much" money. She also files for a waiver because she reported the work.

But she does not bring in any paystubs to prove her case. The monthly wage amounts Burger King put on a letter to Social Security match what Burger King reported to SSA for her 2010 total wages. Therefore, she loses her appeal.

She also loses her waiver request. She did report going to work for Burger King, but not until she'd been there for two months. She also gave wage estimates only half her actual wages, and never reported an increase. Therefore, she is at fault for creating the overpayment.

Same Sex Marriage and the Future of Social Security

(Skip if you bought this book solely for the how-to information.)

I better say first of all I believe consenting adults should have the freedom to do what they will in the bedroom, to live together for a night or a lifetime as they choose. I understand they can love each other and take care of children.

But having worked so long for SSA, I tend to see marriage in financial terms rather than romantic terms (being divorced myself also encourages this viewpoint).

I once heard a debate over same sex marriage SSM) on a radio show, and the first thing the pro SSM speaker said was, "Well, Laura (the host of the show), if you got married and your husband died you'd be protected. We're just asking for the same protection."

"Protection" used this way is a code word for getting money from the Social Security trust funds.

So my bullshit antenna went straight up, and I immediately knew SSM was a money grab no matter how much they talk about love and romance.

I also realized this speaker was not familiar with Social Security rules. He was simply assuming because the radio show host was a woman, she'd get money if her husband died.

Not true.

Study the requirements for spouses and widow(er) benefits as outlined in Chapter 16, and think them through carefully.

For one thing, you'll see the rules hark back to the early days of Social Security when it was assumed most wage earners would be men who had wives and children who would have a great financial need if the working man retired, became disabled or died.

The original spousal benefit categories were just for women. Decades ago they were modified to be gender-neutral.

Although men are now technically eligible, the vast majority of spouse and widow(er) beneficiaries are women. The men who receive are largely men who did not work much under the Social Security system (self-employed and/or in jail and/or just living on a wife who did work under the system).

And you'll see rules that eliminate the benefits if the spouse/widow(er) would get as much or more money on their own Social Security record.

This ensures the only spouses and widow(er)s who receive are those who didn't work as much themselves, and thus were presumably dependent on the income of the wage earner.

Of course, a lot has changed in the past seventy-seven years. The vast majority of women today will get Social Security on their own records, not on a spouse's. The vast majority of women who don't get Social Security on their own records will get a pension from the Post Office, the Civil Service or a state or local government.

And even for those women who are not working as much as their husbands, there are rules about getting on his record.

To get as a widow(er), you have to be age 60. That talk show host was not that old.

To get as a disabled widow(er), you have to be age 50 and disabled within 7 years of the wage earner's death. The talk show host was not that old and obviously not disabled.

If she had a minor child of the wage earner in her care, then she might get mother's benefits. So that is the one Social Security benefit not getting married would bar you from.

I've seen arguments for SSM stating that under the current law their children are not "protected." That's bogus.

Children of a disabled, retired or deceased wage earner have always been protected. Marital status of the parents has no effect on that, and neither does the sexual orientation of either parent.

If you are on a child's birth certificate as their mother or father, or you have legally adopted that child, they are your child and will get SSA if you retire, become disabled or die (assuming you're insured) while they're still minors or if they're disabled before age 22.

If you have a partner who has a child and you want to be counted as that child's parent, then adopt them.

If you're the biological father of a child and not named on the birth certificate, see if you can get it changed, or at least leave behind a notarized statement acknowledging paternity.

Again - sexual orientation of the parents or their marital status does not affect benefits for children. Just have evidence you are the natural or adopted parent of the children.

I have this sneaking suspicion, perhaps because I did work for SSA for over 30 years, some SSM activists believe they're unfairly barred from the Social Security trust funds because they can't legally marry people of the same sex, and they want access to that money.

I suspect they believe once they can legally marry and Social Security is forced to recognize SSM (which it doesn't now, no matter what any state's laws say), there's going to be a bushel of money to party on.

However, the rules for getting spousal and widow(er) benefits are much more stringent than they seem to realize.

I personally resent the idea adult men may draw Social Security checks—while I'm working hard—just because they shared a bed with a man who is now retired, disabled or dead.

Share the bed if you wish, but don't drag my money into it.

I understand the concept of supporting wives and widows who were mainly housewives. I can't emotionally agree with treating a man—no matter what his sexual orientation— as a "housewife."

Adult men who aren't disabled or retired should go to work, not draw checks for having been a "housewife."

However, I suspect it won't happen nearly as much as SSM activists are assuming.

I don't have numbers—I doubt anybody has the necessary combination of sexual orientation attached to earnings record information—but I strongly suspect most gay men and women work as much on average as heterosexuals.

Which means when they apply for spouse and widow(er) benefits, they're going to find out that they're due at least as much on their own earnings record, and therefore not due any spouse or widow(er) benefits despite the legal marital relationship.

Let's Do Away With Dependent Adult Benefits Altogether

The best way to make this fair is to simply recognize in our society today both sexes— no matter what their sexual orientation—work, and do away with the entire concept of dependent benefits for adults.

(As mentioned, children are already protected despite the sexual orientation or marital status of their parents.)

So SSA should simply not pay any dependent adult benefits. Just do away with them. Most adults won't get them anyway, because these days most adults have their own earnings records.

If a woman and her husband agree she can stay home with the kids while he works, that's fine so long as it's a private arrangement between him or her. But why should men and women who are working hard at jobs and businesses subsidize the housewife if her husband becomes disabled, retired or deceased?

Pay the minor children, but let the widow(er)s and spouses go to work so they're insured on their own earnings records.

Let's do away with the entire concept of a spouse or widow(er) receiving benefits on another adult's earnings record.

Then gay men and lesbians could concentrate on getting married for love, not for the (largely) imaginary financial benefits.

The Future...?

(Skip if you bought this book solely for the how-to information.)

In 1950 there were 16 workers in the 5Social Security system per retiree, the life expectancy for 65 year old men was 77, and there were no disability benefits.

Lawmakers assumed the population of the United States would grow on a gradual arithmetic scale. That is, each generation would be slightly larger than the one before it.

A lot has changed. Disability benefits were introduced in 1956 and are now undoubtedly the highest source of program fraud, waste and abuse.

At the end of World War 2, the children of the Great Depression began making babies as if there were no tomorrow. This "baby boomer" generation has warped society and the economy to itself like a neutron star from the very beginning, when it caused the building of thousands of new schools in the 1950s. A few years ago some baby boomers began taking early retirement, and now they're reaching full retirement age.

That's about 80 million people now working who will want to start drawing Social Security RIB benefits by 2031.

In 2007 there were 3.3 workers per retiree, and this is expected to drop to 2.1 by 2035.

Men 65 years old are now expected to live another 16.6 years.

Nobody really knows how the Social Security trust funds are going to deal with this problem. Not only monthly checks are affected, but Medicare and Medicaid (many baby boomers are poor, not wealthy) as well. How can the younger generation pay for all the medical expenses boomers will need?

Nobody knows. And the demographic situation is even worse in much of Europe and Japan.

Currently, most politicians are refusing to face up to the program. President George W. Bush tried to reform the Social Security program, but his proposals were shot down.

A lot of politicians and political advocates are quick to say Social Security in its current form has made many tens of millions of Americans economically secure, so why change it?

It's not sustainable in its current form, but since it was good enough for FDR, it must be good enough for us.

There's no doubt in my mind the program has got to change, and eventually will have to change.

One big solution politically attractive to many politicians in the US is to play the class warfare card. Although it's unfair to tax Social Security benefits, I'm sure that's going to happen more.

Here's why it's unfair and against the original social insurance concept the program was founded on.

Let's compare the twins Joe and George.

Joe and George are completely alike in all ways—except one.

They go to work when they get out of college and make exactly the same amount of money as each other, every year until they retire. They both choose the same month to retire in, so they get exactly the same amount of Social Security benefits—$1,500 per month.

But George has to pay taxes on his Social Security checks. And Joe doesn't. Why not?

Because Joe spends every dime he makes. When he retires, he has no savings and no other source of income. Since his annual Social Security checks add up to only $18,000 and that's his only income, he pays no taxes on them.

However, George is a money saver. He lives a frugal life and invests as much as he can afford into income producing investments, and then reinvests the income from his portfolio.

By the time he retires, he has a large portfolio and receives $100,000 per year in stock dividends, in addition to his Social Security.

Because George was responsible with his money and has income over $25,000, he has to pay taxes on his Social Security checks, even though he receives no more than Joe.

George is better off than Joe, because he chose to be.

But the class war politicians will tell you George doesn't deserve his Social Security benefits because he's rich, while poor Joe is...poor.

But Politicians Will Continue to Erode the Social Insurance System by Making Social Security "Needs Based"—That Is, Welfare

People who have worked hard to save money and invest may be punished by having RIB benefits taken away from them altogether, because they don't "need" it.

The social insurance concept may go the way of the dinosaur and be replaced by Social Security as a national welfare program.

It may not get that bad. I believe the politicians will remove the cap on FICA earnings. That is, you will have to pay 7.65% of all your wages (15.30% of your net profit from self-employment) to the trust funds every year, just as you now do the 1.45% for the Medicare Trust fund.

It's likely that percentage will be raised. Younger people still working won't like that, but they won't have as many votes as the baby boomers.

In return, the full retirement age will be increased. Maybe they'll raise the early retirement age.

Maybe they'll also reduce benefits directly.

I believe increasing the early retirement age and Full Retirement Age makes a lot of sense just because Americans are living so much longer than they were in 1935.

Now, every CR (and ex-CR) knows when the Full Retirement Age goes up, so do DIB claims from people under the Full Retirement Age. And state agency workers tend to favor the claims of people who are so far up in age.

However, this will also be impacted by the trend of living longer and healthier, which shows no sign of stopping, but rather is accelerating as medical science and research advance.

Between nanotechnology and stem cells, there's no telling what is going to happen within the next ten to twenty years just as the trust funds are struggling to pay the baby boomers.

While many baby boomers simply want to sit around and collect checks, many others want a much more active "retirement," if you can even use that word. They want to be free of the corporate jobs they hate, so they can return to some meaningful career they left behind when they stopped being a 25 year old hippie.

It might be teaching disabled children. It might be saving the rain forests. It might be blogging about Jesus.

The fact is, people who take care of themselves now (don't smoke, don't drink too much, exercise moderately, eat well, take nutritious food supplements) can have a very long life.

And I for one wouldn't blame the younger generation for not wanting to work hard to support baby boomers who are still capable of working, even if they're 68, 98 or 198 years old.

The good news is this will also impact disability rolls. One thing we should do is stop patronizing people with certain medical conditions. Many disability "advocates" want disabled people treated like everybody else (such as required by the Americans with Disabilities Act), but then want to keep them eligible for special benefits nobody else receives.

Although many people say Social Security's medical requirements are extremely tough, I'm skeptical of that, at least in some categories. I know from experience the first thing many people do after spending their DIB and SSI back money is they go out and get a job.

I'm all for education and vocational training helping people found to be disabled. But I've seen many disabled people who have no trouble getting work even WITHOUT additional schooling or vocational training.

If SSA's disability standards are so tough to meet, how come so many people found disabled under those standards can go to work without any help? It's not unusual for SSI people to be found disabled, then go out and get the best job they've ever had in their life.

However, no politician of either party wants to look like the blue meanie oppressing the disabled, so none of them will touch this issue with a ten foot pole.

NOTE: just this week a politician asked the agency to look into the case of an SSI recipient who was choosing to live as an adult baby. Yet he was able to drive to the hardware store to purchase materials and make his own crib.

This is a sign disability may not be as "untouchable" as I originally thought—especially people who allege medical problems that don't attract sympathy.

My hope though is in years to come medical science will be able to help more people recover from injuries and diseases so they don't meet SSA requirements.

That will mean more people working and paying into the system, and fewer people collecting monthly checks.

Eventually it will mean the end of both disability and retirement as we know those concepts today

Final Words

You now the information you need to file for either retirement and disability and have the best chance of success.

If you do what I've told you:

Tell the truth, the whole truth and nothing but the truth.

Be organized, prepared with all your work and medical information, including the date of entitlement (for RIB claims) or date of onset (for DIB claims).

Have all the medical proofs and forms you can turn in.

Have all nonmedical proofs ready, such as relationship proofs and proof of your income and resources if filing for SSI.

Keep your address and telephone number up to date, and read your mail from Social Security the same day you receive it.

Attend your consultative exam.

If denied, file your appeal immediately so the CR does not have to waste their scarce time writing up a "good cause" determination.

Your CR and state agency counselor will love you! You'll be their dream claimant. If everybody had been so diligent about their applications and the checks, maybe I'd still be a CR.

Remember the easier and faster you make things for your CR and state agency counselor, the faster you get a decision—which means a check for you if you're approved.

I cannot guarantee you will be approved, of course. But doing the above things will speed up your decision and give you the best chance possible.

Good luck in all aspects of your life.